the
organic
kitchen

the
organic
kitchen

a cook's guide to natural ingredients
with over 40 delicious recipes

ysanne spevack

southwater

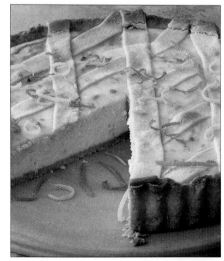

Dedicated to my mum, Coral,
for all her inspiration both in and out of the kitchen,
to Steve, for his support throughout the writing of this book,
and to John at the Organic Delivery Company, for his fantastic fruit and veg.

This edition is published by Southwater

Southwater is an imprint of Anness Publishing Ltd
Hermes House, 88–89 Blackfriars Road, London SE1 8HA
tel. 020 7401 2077; fax 020 7633 9499

www.southwaterbooks.com; www.annesspublishing.com

If you like the images in this book and would like to investigate using them for publishing, promotions or advertising, please visit our website www.practicalpictures.com for more information.

UK agent: The Manning Partnership Ltd; tel. 01225 478444; fax 01225 478440;
sales@manning-partnership.co.uk

UK distributor: Grantham Book Services Ltd; tel. 01476 541080; fax 01476 541061;
orders@gbs.tbs-ltd.co.uk

North American agent/distributor: National Book Network; tel. 301 459 3366; fax 301 429 5746;
www.nbnbooks.com

Australian agent/distributor: Pan Macmillan Australia; tel. 1300 135 113; fax 1300 135 103;
customer.service@macmillan.com.au

New Zealand agent/distributor: David Bateman Ltd; tel. (09) 415 7664; fax (09) 415 8892

Publisher: *Joanna Lorenz*
Editor: *Elizabeth Woodland*
Production Controller: *Darren Price*
Project Editor: *Joy Wotton*
Photographers: *Peter Anderson and Simon Smith*

ETHICAL TRADING POLICY
At Anness Publishing we believe that business should be conducted in an ethical and ecologically sustainable way, with respect for the environment and a proper regard to the replacement of the natural resources we employ.
As a publisher, we use a lot of wood pulp to make high-quality paper for printing, and that wood commonly comes from spruce trees. We are therefore currently growing more than 750,000 trees in three Scottish forest plantations: Berrymoss (130 hectares/320 acres), West Touxhill (125 hectares/305 acres) and Deveron Forest (75 hectares/185 acres). The forests we manage contain more than 3.5 times the number of trees employed each year in making paper for the books we manufacture.
Because of this ongoing ecological investment programme, you, as our customer, can have the pleasure and reassurance of knowing that a tree is being cultivated on your behalf to naturally replace the materials used to make the book you are holding.
Our forestry programme is run in accordance with the UK Woodland Assurance Scheme (UKWAS) and will be certified by the internationally recognized Forest Stewardship Council (FSC). The FSC is a non-government organization dedicated to promoting responsible management of the world's forests. Certification ensures forests are managed in an environmentally sustainable and socially responsible way. For further information about this scheme, go to www.annesspublishing.com/trees

A CIP catalogue record for this book is available from the British Library.

Previously published as part of a larger volume, *The Organic Cookbook*

NOTES
Bracketed terms are for American readers. For all recipes, quantities are given in both metric and imperial measures and, where appropriate, measures are also given in standard cups and spoons. Follow one set, but not a mixture because they are not interchangeable. Standard spoon and cup measures are level. 1 tsp = 5ml, 1 tbsp = 15ml, 1 cup = 250ml/8fl oz. Australian standard tablespoons are 20ml. Australian readers shoud use 3 tsp in place of 1 tbsp for measuring small quantities of gelatine, cornflour, salt etc. Medium (US large) eggs are used unless otherwise stated.

PUBLISHER'S NOTE
Although the advice and information in this book are believed to be accurate and true at the time of going to press, neither the authors nor the publisher can accept any legal responsibility or liability for any errors or omissions that may be made.

CONTENTS

INTRODUCTION

Organic food is the fastest growing sector of the entire food industry. Step into any supermarket and you will see an impressive array of organic produce, not tucked away at the end of an aisle, but proudly and prominently displayed. This is often the first point of contact for shoppers unfamiliar with organic food, but having experienced the superior flavours and learned of the undeniable health benefits, many people go on to investigate box schemes, farmers' markets featuring organic produce and small, local organic suppliers.

Interest in organic food and farming is at an all-time high. This is partly due to the fact that people are better informed about nutrition, more concerned about the environment and more cautious about the short- and long-term effects of diet on health than at any time in the past, but there are also more fundamental reasons, such as flavour. To put it simply, we appreciate good food. This generation is more widely travelled than any previous one, and is discovering

Below: Organic sheep and lambs graze on unsprayed grass, free from pesticides.

exotic cuisines and exciting new tastes from all over the world. People eat out more, and are more adventurous when cooking at home. As palates become increasingly sophisticated, we demand more from the ingredients that make up our meals, so it is hardly surprising that we increasingly favour organic food.

But What Is Organic Food?

Organic farming is the cultivation of crops and rearing of livestock with natural soil fertility at the heart of the system. Organic farmers believe that by working hard to maintain and encourage good soil structure on their land, the crops and livestock grown and bred there will flourish. They work with nature, rather than trying to bend nature to their purpose, so produce is grown without the routine use of pesticides or artificial fertilizers, and animals are reared without being treated with growth promoters or unnecessarily dosed with antibiotics.

If this sounds like a return to the way things used to be, it is, but only to a point. Modern organic farming is highly scientific and makes considerable use of

Above: Organic pumpkins and squash are grown free from artificial fertilizers.

technology. Research into more efficient organic farming methods is ongoing. For food to be labelled organic, it must have been produced according to strict guidelines, which are rigidly regulated.

Soil fertility is promoted by crop rotation, composting and planting crops that supply specific nutrients. Farmers encourage predator insects such as ladybirds (ladybugs) to visit by planting their favourite flowers. They may also sometimes introduce other predators to control pests biologically. When coupled with preventative methods, such as growing in polytunnels, where insects can be kept out, the need to use agrochemical pesticides is avoided.

Agrochemical Farming

The cultivation of crops and rearing of livestock using agrochemicals was first promoted on a large scale in the 1950s, in response to widespread food shortages during and immediately after World War II. This was a period of modernism, with technologies of all kinds being optimistically embraced. Agrochemicals held the promise of maximizing food production, so they were universally adopted. They achieved

Right: Organic cattle are less susceptible to disease because they are always free-range and have access to the outdoors.

their immediate objectives, but at a cost to the environment that is only now beginning to be fully appreciated.

Yields from organic and agrochemical farms are now almost identical, and organic yields continue to grow as a result of continued research into intensive organic agriculture. Organic farmers also benefit from access to much wider seed banks than those customarily used by agrochemical farmers, so can select the best varieties of crops for their climate and terrain.

Organic farming now utilizes some of the same non-invasive technology as agrochemical farming. Satellites, for example, are used to predict weather patterns or map insect migrations.

The Cost of Going Organic
If yields are improving and organic food production is becoming steadily more efficient, why does organic food tend to cost more than agrochemical food? The answer lies in outdated government subsidy schemes, which are based on the aspirations and knowledge of post-World War II policymakers. Agrochemical farmers receive a much higher amount of taxpayers' money than organic farmers. Historically, this was because farmers were encouraged to experiment with chemicals to increase yields. Thinking has changed radically since those days, but subsidizing policy has not altered for the last fifty years.

Farmers are actively encouraged to spray their fields with chemical pesticides and fertilizers. When these chemicals run off farms and pollute the water table, huge sums of money must be spent internationally in clean-up operations. It is not the chemical companies or the farmers who pay for this pollution management; it is the taxpayer.

Consumers pay for agrochemical products three times. First at the checkout, then – about half the price of the item again – through taxes as a subsidy to agrochemical farmers, and

finally through further taxes to clean up the water table. This economic breakdown does not include any costs incurred to industry through the ill health of agrochemical farm workers who have been exposed to toxins.

Organic food will continue to be marginally more expensive than agrochemical food until government policies change. However, the difference in food quality that organic food offers more than justifies this price premium. An organic apple contains more vitamins, minerals and phytonutrients than a non-organic apple. It also contains about 25 per cent less water. It is likely to be a more interesting variety, will almost certainly taste better and will have a

more enjoyable texture. Most importantly, it will not be coated in an untested cocktail of up to twenty artificial chemicals and waxes.

Organic Livestock
Animal welfare is a fundamental principle of organic livestock, poultry and dairy farming. Organic animals are always free range. Because they have access to the outdoors and are not intensively reared in enclosed spaces, they are less susceptible to disease and, although farmers will take appropriate action if an animal becomes unwell, there is no need for the routine administration of antibiotics that is standard preventative practice on agrochemical farms.

Above: *These dairy cows are being reared organically, free from hormones that increase milk production or encourage growth.*

Organic farmers will often use such complementary medicines as homeopathic treatments to cure a sick animal and inject antibiotics only as a last resort when other treatments have failed.

Organic farmers are not allowed to use hormones to encourage animal growth or increase milk production. In countries where growth hormones such as BST (bovine somatotropin) are administered, dairy cows often suffer intense pain from unnaturally swollen udders. Their milk – and dairy products produced from it – contains the same hormones, increasing the consumer's risk of multi-generational cancers and hormone disruption disorders.

Fish
Organic fish, whether wild or farmed, should come from sustainable fisheries and farms, and be caught using fishing practices that protect the environment.
Wild Fish Logic dictates that all wild fish are organic, since they swim and eat where they will. However, pollution, insensitive fishing methods and proximity to major shipping lanes all have a detrimental effect on wild fish stocks, and there is no standard for organics in wild fish. The Marine Stewardship Council is an international organization offering an accreditation scheme for sustainable wild fisheries.
Farmed Fish The conditions under which fish are farmed vary widely. For farmed fish to be labelled organic, they must be reared responsibly. This means giving them adequate room to move, letting them grow and develop naturally and giving them organic feed. This is not the case on many agrochemical fish farms, where fish populations can be so high and intensive that infestation and disease are commonplace and chemical pesticides must be used liberally to control them. Pesticides, waste fish food and sewage from agrochemical fish farms frequently pollute our rivers and waterways, and it is not just these substances that escape. Fish get under the wire, too, and in many European rivers, four out of every five salmon caught originated on an agrochemical farm.

Farmed fish are bred to mature later and be less aggressive than their wild counterparts in order to produce a greater yield and be easier to manage.

The damage from wild and farmed salmon interbreeding is immense, with natural fish stocks at ever increasing risk. Intensive fish farms are beginning to address these problems in many areas of the world, but to be sure that your farmed fish is produced responsibly, make sure it carries the mark of an organic certification body that you trust.

Hemp
This is a wonder crop that puts more nutrients back into the soil than it needs to grow. It is therefore ideal for farmers who are converting their land to organic methods. The conversion period required for organic certification can be a difficult time financially for farmers. While the land is renewing itself, farmers may not sell their produce as organic even though they are not using agrochemicals. Hemp can usefully bridge the gap by providing a saleable crop while improving soil fertility.

The applications of hemp are extraordinary. The ropes and sails used on the ships that first charted our seas were made of hemp. So was the first pair of Levi's jeans. Hemp also made the paper on which the original American Constitution was written. Hemp is the most versatile organic crop we have.

Below: *Organic fish are farmed with care for the environment.*

Above: *Organic fruit contains more vitamins, minerals and phytonutrients than non-organic fruit. It also tastes better.*

You can make cosmetics from its oil, power cars with it, and even use it for making plastics. In fact, hemp can do anything that a hydrocarbon can do. In these times of dwindling fossil fuel reserves, hemp is potentially a major part of the solution because it actually reduces greenhouse gases plus it manufactures oxygen when it grows, and can easily be processed into a powerful fuel source to rival oil.

Hemp seed is the only complete vegetable protein known, with a nutritional make-up that is even more balanced than soya. Sixty-five per cent of the protein in hemp is in globular edestin form, which is the most easily digestible form of protein. The oil content of hemp seeds typically consists of 60 per cent Omega-6; 20 per cent Omega-3 and 10 per cent Omega essential fatty acids (EFAs). This is seen as the most suitable ratio of dietary fat for long-term human consumption. Hemp seed oil also contains GLA, which is the active constituent of evening primrose oil. This makes the oil ideal for the treatment of PMS, eczema, joint conditions and even some cancers.

Left: *Hemp products include such beauty products as soaps, moisturizers and loofah-like scrubs.*

NOT EVERYTHING ORGANIC IS FOOD!

Non-organic cotton and tobacco are two pesticide-dependent crops grown widely in the Americas and in developing countries. Dangers to the consumer from agrochemicals used in the cultivation of non-food crops are minimal, but when the soil's natural fertility is undermined by artificial fertilizers, farmers become reliant on agrochemicals. Concerns are high for farm workers in developing countries exposed to pesticides deemed too strong for use on food crops. Where protective clothing is absent, they have a higher than average incidence of cancers and respiratory conditions. There is also a high rate of early mortality among the farmers themselves.

Organic cotton and tobacco are available. The Scandinavian Oeko-Tex mark is an assurance that fabrics are organic or sustainable. The American Spirit tobacco company manufactures organic cigarettes.

Seeds and garden flowers are two more areas of environmental concern. Because it is vital that no weed seeds contaminate the product, agrochemical seed producers spray their crops liberally with herbicides.

Cut flowers are not regulated as stringently as food crops, so farm workers and the environment can lose out. Buying organically grown flowers benefits both the people who grew them and the planet.

Organically grown hyacinths

WHY GO ORGANIC?

There are dozens – many would say hundreds – of excellent reasons for choosing the organic option. Apart from benefits to the individual in terms of health, avoidance of chemicals and the sheer enjoyment of eating food that is full of flavour, there are environmental issues to consider, as well as moral questions such as animal welfare, the health of farm workers and fair trade.

Improved Health

All organic food is better for you than the non-organic equivalent. Fresh organic produce contains more vitamins, minerals, enzymes and other micro-nutrients than intensively farmed produce. Organic fruit and vegetables are full of juice and flavour, and there are many different

Below: Organic cauliflower, cabbage, broccoli and Brussels sprouts are high in glucosinolates, which help prevent cancer.

varieties to try. Organic meat, poultry and dairy produce are of excellent quality and usually lower in saturated fat.

Vitamins and Minerals The reason why fresh organic produce contains more vitamins and minerals than the agrochemical equivalent is largely due to the method of cultivation. Unlike agrochemical fruit and vegetables, which are sprayed with artificial fertilizers that force the plants to grow quickly, even in inferior soil, organic fruit and vegetables are allowed to grow and ripen more naturally in richer soil, obtaining the maximum variety of micronutrients.

These micronutrients are also more concentrated in organic fruit and vegetables, because they contain much less water than agrochemical produce.

Phytonutrients Organic produce is rich in naturally occurring chemical compounds known as phytonutrients. These are found in fresh fruit and vegetables and

help to fight disease and promote good health. More research is needed to pinpoint the precise benefits of all these compounds, but much is already known. Glucosinolates in cabbage, broccoli, cauliflower and Brussels sprouts help to prevent cancer. Flavonoids are powerful antioxidants. The strongest flavonoids are found in onions and garlic. Eating onions and garlic regularly significantly reduces the risk of heart disease and the spread of cancer.

While all fresh produce contains phytonutrients, organic produce contains more than its non-organic equivalent. This is because all plants produce phytonutrients as part of their natural defence against pests. If a plant is protected from pests by agrochemicals, there is no need for it to produce phytochemicals in the same quantity. Also, studies have found that when plants take up high levels of nitrogen from the soil, they produce

Above: *Just some of the fruits available organically: apples, grapes, pineapple, oranges, kiwi fruit and passion fruit.*

fewer and less diverse phytonutrients. Agrochemical crops are liberally sprayed with nitrogen fertilizers to make them grow quicker, whereas organic crops are grown in more balanced and less nitrogen-rich soil.

Fats Hydrogenated fats are oils that have had hydrogen added to them so that they become solid or semi-solid at room temperature. They are widely used in the food industry despite the fact that nutritionists universally agree that they are a major co-factor in heart disease, cancer, diabetes and obesity. The surest way to remove hydrogenated fats from your diet is to go organic. Organic food regulations throughout the world prohibit the use of hydrogenated fats.

Eating too much saturated fat is a contributing factor in cardiovascular diseases such as heart attacks and stroke. Saturated fat is present in organic beef as well as in intensively reared beef, but the percentage is likely to be lower. Saturated fat is also easier to remove from organic beef. In intensively reared

cattle saturated fat is more evenly distributed, so is harder to cut away when you are preparing the meat for cooking. Since it clogs up your arteries, the more saturated fat you can remove from your food the better.

Meat, poultry, eggs and milk from grass-fed animals also contain more conjugated linoleic acid or CLA. This substance helps those who consume it to maintain a healthy weight, and studies have shown that it reduces the risk of heart disease and may help to prevent cancer. So although organic meat contains saturated fat, it also contains CLA to balance it.

The Balanced Diet
A wholesome, organic diet provides balanced nutrition, including a healthy range of vitamins, minerals and phytonutrients. This is an important consideration in a world where many people opt for convenience foods that are

often high in fat and sugar and offer little in terms of nutrition. The body craves the nutrients it lacks, and this can drive people to overeat, yet remain malnourished. There is a direct correlation between over-consumption malnutrition trends in industrialized nations and eating non-organic food. Obesity epidemics have occurred in countries that rely on agrochemicals to grow and process their foods.

Improved Immunity There is evidence to suggest that people who eat organic food build up a stronger immunity to disease than those who consistently eat food that is laden with chemicals. Eating over-processed, non-organic junk food puts a strain on immune systems already compromised by living in a polluted world, by forcing the liver and kidneys to work harder to remove the toxins they frequently contain.

A New Zealand report into the possible benefits of an organic diet suggested that people who follow an organic diet benefit from a very marked decline in influenza and experienced far fewer colds and catarrhal problems than other members of the population. Further reported benefits included clear, healthy skin, improved dental health and excellent general health.

Below: *Organic eggs are high in linoleic acid, which helps maintain a healthy weight.*

Above: *Eating an organic diet before conception and during pregnancy will help rid the body of toxins.*

Increased Fertility Studies appear to support a link between organic diets and increased fertility in men. The World Health Organization estimates that the average sperm count for male adults is about 66 million/ml. Two recent studies recorded that men who eat organic food have between 99 and 127 million sperm/ml. More research is needed to confirm these findings. However, the fact that a balanced organic diet is more nutritionally sound and contains fewer chemicals or artificial hormones than a non-organic diet, is bound to offer the best option for men – and women – wanting to support their sexual health and improve their chances of conceiving.

Avoiding the Chemical Cocktail

The average adult living in one of the industrialized nations has between 300 and 500 agrochemical pesticides in his or her body at any one time. Each of these toxic chemicals is stored in body fat, and each is toxic enough to kill insects. In combination, they are certainly more poisonous. Pesticides can remain stored in body fat for many years. No long-term studies have truly evaluated the damage to our health that these chemicals pose, but there is evidence to suggest that they exacerbate chronic conditions and seriously undermine health.

Children are particularly susceptible to agrochemical toxins. They have a higher intake of food than adults in relation to their body weight, and their bodies are less efficient at eliminating toxins. Breast milk from mothers whose diets are not organic generally contains concentrations of pesticides. These have been shown to adversely affect brain development in babies. Ideally, a woman planning to conceive a child should adopt an organic diet at least one year before becoming pregnant. This gives her body time to detoxify, helping to create a healthier environment for the foetus to grow in and then purer breast milk for the baby once it has been born.

Artificial Additives Every year, the average American eats more than two kilograms of chemical food additives. Seven thousand artificial additives are permitted to be used in conventional food. Only seven of these – the most innocuous – are allowed to be used in processed organic food. Artificial additives are used by manufacturers to improve the shelf life, flavour, colour, sweetness and saltiness of non-organic

Below: *Organic fruit and vegetables, on sale at a local farmers' market, are fresh and full of goodness.*

processed foods. Flavour enhancers may be added to disguise inferior quality ingredients. Although some artificial additives are absolutely harmless, many undermine our health. Generally they are used in combination, unleashing an unresearched toxic combination upon the consumer, which may well have implications in terms of cancer, asthma, liver disease and osteoporosis.

When food deteriorates naturally, you can see at a glance when it is past its best. Preservatives may artificially prolong a food's shelf life, but they do not prolong the life of all the nutrients within the product. When preservatives are banned, as in processed organic food, you can be sure that as long as the food is fresh, it is full of goodness. **Antibiotics and Hormones** Intensively reared livestock are routinely fed and injected with antibiotics to keep them healthy. These substances pass into their meat. People who eat this meat develop reduced immunity through over-exposure to antibiotics. On the other hand, bacteria that become over-exposed to antibiotics become increasingly resistant to them. The British Medical Association has stated that: "The risk to human health of antibiotic resistance…is one of the major health threats that could be faced in the 21st century."

Hormones and endocrine disrupting chemicals (EDCs) also pose a threat to health. Five out of the twelve most commonly used pesticides in the world are known to be EDCs. This means that they are known to affect the delicate balance of human hormones. Women in Hawaii have an extremely high rate of breast cancer. Hawaii also has a high rate of zeno-oestrogens from pesticides in its groundwater. A Danish scientific study, which tracked more than seven hundred Hawaiian women over twenty years, concluded that there is a probable link between the pesticides in the water and breast cancers.

There is also evidence that growth hormones from intensively farmed meat can lead to a wide variety of human endocrine disorders, from obesity to multi-generational cancers.

Food Safety

All organic animals that are naturally vegetarian are fed only vegetarian food. This was a huge benefit during the UK's BSE (Bovine Spongiform Encephalopathy) crisis. BSE was caused and spread because cows were fed contaminated food, which was itself animal in origin. All organic farms in the UK are completely BSE-free because organic cows are always fed food that is 100 per cent vegetarian.

Organic meat and dairy produce is free from genetically modified organisms or GMOs because all food for organic animals must be GMO-free by law. The diet of organic animals is also solvent free. This may seem obvious until it is considered that non-organic animals regularly eat food contaminated with solvents. Non-organic cooking oil is usually produced by soaking oil-rich vegetable matter in solvents. The oil is then extracted from the liquid, and the remaining solid matter is used for animal feed. Solvent-extracted animal feed is banned from organic farms.

Natural Flavours

During the year 2000, 43 per cent of consumers who bought organic food in Britain declared that they did so because they thought it tasted better

Above: Heirloom and rare varieties of potatoes are appearing at markets as organic farmers seek out new crops.

than non-organic food. Tastes vary from person to person, but there are sound reasons why organic food tastes better.

Most agrochemical crops are grown from seeds bred to produce a high yield. Organic fresh produce, however, comes from seeds bred primarily for flavour. Many organic farmers take pride in growing heirloom crops. These crops were once highly prized but have been overlooked in recent years because they were less commercially profitable than modern varieties. Organic growers in industrialized nations regularly produce about a hundred different kinds of potato. This is considerably fewer than the thousand or more varieties on sale at the farmer's market in the town of Cuzco in Peru, but at least five times more than the twenty or so varieties of agrochemically grown potatoes on sale in the USA or UK.

The slower growth rates of organic crops allow more time for flavour to develop naturally. Phytonutrients often help to flavour the fresh produce in which they occur so, as well as being good for health, high levels of certain

Above: Flowers planted among vegetables encourage the predator insects that control pests in an environmentally friendly fashion.

phytonutrients boost the taste factor. Sugar levels are often slightly higher in organic fresh produce than in non-organic varieties; this is particularly obvious in carrots and apples. Organic fruit is more likely to be allowed to ripen naturally on the tree, granting more time for flavours and sweetness to develop.

The lower percentage of water in organic fresh produce concentrates the nutrients and intensifies the flavour. If you were to evaporate all the water from an agrochemical carrot and an organic carrot of equal weight, the remaining dry matter from the organic carrot would be some 26 per cent heavier.

Food animals raised organically also benefit from growing more slowly than their agrochemical equivalents, and their meat becomes more flavoursome during the process. Another reason why meat from organic farms tastes better is because flavour is an important factor in selecting which type of animal to raise, and farmers are increasingly choosing the

Right: Fresh produce grown in an organic vegetable garden is an excellent option for the health-conscious consumer.

traditional heritage breeds that are noted for the tastiness of their meat above yield.

Organic prepared foods are allowed to contain very few of the chemical flavourings and flavour enhancers found in non-organic foods. Monosodium glutamate, for instance, is outlawed in organic food. This substance, commonly known as MSG, has been linked to nausea, dizziness and even asthma attacks. Organic foods taste so good that they do not need flavour enhancers.

Although much organic produce is currently grown a long way from the point of sale, it is best to buy it fresh from local producers. Not only will it have the finest flavour and highest concentration of nutrients, it will not contribute to pollution by having to be transported long distances. The range of fruit and vegetables may not be as great as that on offer in supermarkets, but the pleasure of enjoying seasonal treats such as strawberries in summer is more than adequate compensation.

Animal Welfare

Organic farm animals and poultry are treated with respect, without recourse to artificial hormones, antibiotics or routine drug therapies. Inhumane practices such as battery farming are banned. Dairy cows raised organically

have, on average, 50 per cent more room in their barns than non-organic cows, and unlike the latter, they are always provided with bedding. They also enjoy much more time out of doors. The same holds true for organic poultry.

Wildlife and the Environment

Our environment is under immense threat. Over the last 30 years, intensive farming in many countries has led to dramatic erosion of the soil. Bird populations have declined by up to 70 per cent, and some species of butterflies, frogs, grass snakes and wild mammals have been brought near extinction. Wild flowers and shrubs that once flourished in the fields are now seldom seen. Intensive farmers grub up ancient hedgerows that surround their fields to allow access for their giant machinery.

Organic farmers actively promote biodiversity by cherishing hedges, not just for their natural beauty, but for the practical support they offer. They play a vital role in supplying a habitat for the birds and insects that an organic farm needs in order to function. Wild flowers at the edge of a field attract butterflies and useful predators to the crop, so organic farmers always keep a strip of wild land around a field. Intensive farmers destroy resources such as these, either mechanically or by using

Above: A willow fence forms a natural field boundary and encourages butterflies.

pesticides. Many chemical pesticides are directly related to nerve gases. They are designed to kill. Those pests that survive being drenched with pesticides may develop immunity. Stronger pesticides must be developed and this leads to an ever-increasing cycle.

Although agrochemical farmers use pesticides to target specific pests, they are toxic to many creatures. Small mammals and birds are often killed or weakened by agricultural pesticides. Equally damaging are agrochemical seeds that have been treated with organochlorides in an attempt to prevent them being eaten. These highly poisonous chemicals, which last for years in the environment, kill numerous birds and animals every year.

Chemicals sprayed on crops eventually either penetrate the plants or trickle down into the soil, polluting the land and draining into the water table. The poisons then flow into streams and rivers, polluting the ecosystem. Agrochemical fertilizers are just as damaging to the ecosystem as pesticides. Nitrate-based fertilizers also seep out of the fields into the water system. In rivers and lakes, they stimulate the growth of algae. Excessive algae throws the whole ecosystem out of balance, poisoning waterways.

Farm Workers' Health and Fair Trade

On agrochemical farms, especially those in such developing countries as India, workers are often at direct risk from pesticide pollution. Protective clothing and machinery is expensive, whereas pesticide chemicals are relatively cheap. The result is that many farm workers are forced to apply these poisons to crops while unprotected. It is not only the farm workers themselves who are at risk – pesticides also endanger the general population.

Many farm workers in developing nations are exposed to horrifying amounts of poisons every day from childhood onwards. Pesticide exposure can lead to multi-generational diseases and cancers. The children of farm workers are more likely to have genetic defects that continue to successive generations. The workers often receive only subsistence wages for working long and back-breakingly hard days. In some countries, the average age of death for farm workers is around fifty.

Going organic avoids supporting these types of injustices. Using spending power sensitively is a direct way of working towards a fairer trading world. Many organic products are fairly traded, which means that a buyer will offer a reasonable price for crops. The majority

of trading between the developed and the developing world does not currently follow this principle. A cash-poor farmer may be forced to sell his crop for less than its worth because he does not have the bargaining power of a multinational company. For assurance that an organic product is fairly traded, look out for the Fairtrade seal and consult your supplier or shopkeeper.

Packaging

While packaging provides a valuable method of food preservation without the use of additives, unnecessary packaging is wasteful and environmentally insensitive. Many smaller organic companies are beginning to use recycled and recyclable containers for their products, but too many organic foods are still wrapped in the same plastics and bleached non-recycled papers as non-organic products.

Lobbying these organic companies to change their practices can help, but it is equally vital that organic consumers make every effort to recycle their waste. Glass, aluminium and paper are all candidates for recycling. Paper and plastic bags can be reused, and a compost bin is valuable for disposing of waste organic matter.

Below: Recycling organic waste matter in compost bins is good for the environment and enriches the soil of any garden.

THE ORGANIC KITCHEN

The organic cook has a vast array of ingredients, from fresh fruit and vegetables to fine quality meat and store-cupboard staples. Take the same care with preparation as you do with selection and storage and you'll be rewarded with delicious dishes. Exploring the range of organic fresh and store-cupboard items is a rewarding experience. If you buy fresh produce direct from the grower, ask the names of varieties so you can seek out your favourites. The selection that follows is not intended to be an exhaustive guide to every organic item, but it does introduce some of the best buys from organic growers and producers around the world.

FRESH PRODUCE

Good fruit and vegetables are at the heart of organic cuisine. The main point of agreement between health experts and nutritionists throughout the world is that we need to eat more fruit and vegetables. The United Nations World Health Organization has stated that if you eat five portions of fresh produce every day, you halve your chances of getting cancer.

If you can't afford to buy organic produce every day, it is better for you to supplement your diet with non-organic alternatives than to cut back on fruit and vegetables. Organic fresh produce is, however, nutritionally richer, tastier and more diverse. As well as the usual varieties on sale, you will find rare heirloom types of fruit and vegetables.

There is a huge global market for both organic and agrochemical produce,

Below: Stock up on fresh organic vegetables at local farmers' markets.

and imported fruit and vegetables often travel thousands of miles before they reach our shores. Because demand for organic produce is growing at such a high rate in industrialized countries, many organic fruit and vegetables are likely to have been transported long distances.

Local Produce

If you can get it, it is better to buy locally grown produce. There are two main reasons why this is superior to imported organic fruit and vegetables: nutrition and the need to avoid increasing pollution.

Locally grown food is more nutritious than food that has been flown in from another country. Fruit and vegetables for export are often picked before they are fully ripe and kept chilled to avoid spoilage. This means that they fail to develop the complex flavours and nutritional compounds available in produce that has been allowed to ripen naturally and has been freshly picked

Above: Growing your own organic herbs will add taste and nutrition to your cooking.

and transported no further than to the nearest farmers' market. Also, organic standards vary in different countries. Some are not as stringent as others in terms of conversion periods from agrochemical to organic farming, or in nurturing natural soil fertility.

The other major advantage of buying locally grown organic produce is to avoid contributing to pollution. Long-distance transportation of food, whether it be organic or agrochemical, currently uses enormous quantities of petrochemicals, to fuel aeroplanes, ships or road vehicles. Burning fossil fuels is the antithesis of the organic ideal. Major ecological advances, such as fuel cell technology, are in the pipeline for green transportation. However, as long as petrochemicals power organic food imports, it is preferable to buy locally grown organic produce where possible.

That said, buying imported organic fruit is sometimes the only option. Citrus trees do not grow outdoors in cool climates, and date palms prefer arid climates to wet ones. Supplementing locally grown organic produce in season with the occasional imported organic treat is probably a good balance for most organic connoisseurs.

Growing and Buying

The best way to take advantage of the hundreds of different varieties of organic fruit and vegetables is to grow your own. Whether you have a couple of tubs on the patio, a vegetable plot or an impressive garden, preparing the soil,

Above: Freshly dug organic potatoes have a flavour all of their own.

nurturing the plants and then reaping the harvest is richly rewarding. The pleasures of gardening aside, the fresher the produce, the tastier and more nutritious it will be.

If you don't have green fingers, the best way to ensure that vegetables and fruit are fresh is to buy them from a local farmers' market or through a box scheme. Such schemes are operated by small individual growers or co-operatives. Customers opt for regular deliveries, either specifying which seasonal vegetables and fruit they would like to receive, or paying a fixed amount each week and leaving the selection of produce to the grower. The arrival of the box is then a delightful surprise, and often there will be extra treats, such as a few fresh herbs, a small box of berries or a head of the new season's garlic.

Buying Direct

One key benefit of buying fruit and vegetables direct from the grower is to maintain a valid connection with our food. Purchasing vegetables from the man who grew them allows information about the produce to be exchanged. Stories about an individual crop can be passed on and cooking tips and recipes shared. A farmer might also welcome feedback on a new variety that he is experimenting with, and customers can let him know which fruit or vegetables they have particularly enjoyed.

Children who have watched carrots being lifted or have sifted through sacks of potatoes with soil still clinging to them, will soon make the connection between their food and the place it comes from, and will be much more likely to enjoy their organic greens.

Farmers get a much better deal selling their organic food directly. Not only do they obtain about double the price at a farmers' market than they would if they sold to the supermarket, but they enjoy the contact with the townsfolk who tuck into their produce. Never before has the connection between urban and rural societies been so weak. Farmers' markets and box schemes help to bridge the gap.

Supermarkets

It is possible, of course, to shop at the supermarket. While it is heartening that supermarkets are providing greater access to organic fresh produce than before, it is useful to be aware of a couple of negative aspects. Supermarkets generally spray non-organic produce with pesticides after it has left the field to ensure that stores remain free of insects. And, to avoid contamination of organic produce, they have to protect it in plastic packaging. This does not alter the organic status of the produce but the packaging does contribute to the environmental pollution that organic farming techniques aim to minimize. With increased public pressure, larger supermarket chains are likely to address this issue.

Another point to consider is that of food miles. Supermarkets tend to pool their products at central depots. This makes for easier distribution, but can be very wasteful of fuel and energy. An organic potato grown near Town A might well be driven to a central washing plant hundreds of miles away, near Town B. It may then be driven to the central supermarket distribution depot a similar distance away in Town C, only to be transported back to Town A for sale in the supermarket there.

Right: Some packaging, such as this mug and spoon made out of recycled paper, is not harmful to the environment.

CONVENIENCE FOODS

Enthusiastic organic cooks would doubtless prefer always to buy and cook fresh ingredients, but there are occasions when it is useful to have ready-made meals and frozen foods to hand. The wide range of organic convenience foods extends to pasta sauces, soups, TV dinners and freshly prepared sandwiches.

Organic convenience products are unlikely to be as tasty or nutritionally balanced as organic foods prepared at home, but they are better for you than the non-organic alternative. They contain only a small number of artificial additives and are prohibited from containing hydrogenated fats. Such foods may not be irradiated and are not allowed to contain genetically modified ingredients.

Many non-organic processed foods contain excessive levels of refined white sugar and salt, both of which should be avoided. The quick energy rush provided by white sugar is followed always by energy depletion. Complex natural unrefined sweeteners, such as organic fruit syrups, produce a far more balanced response from the body. Too much salt raises blood pressure, increasing the risk of heart disease and strokes. The majority of organic prepared foods offer a safe level of salt, but it is important to check the salt and sugar content on the label of all convenience products.

The good news is that some convenience foods, such as frozen organic fruit and vegetables, can be more nutritious than the fresh non-organic equivalent. This is because produce is frozen within hours of being picked, whereas fresh non-organic produce may have been picked many days before.

Storing Fresh Fruit and Vegetables

It is very important to store organic produce carefully because it will not keep as long as non-organic examples.

Store ripe fruit in a cool place, away from direct sunlight. Green bananas will ripen within a couple of days if they are stored in a plastic bag with an over-ripe banana. Soft fruits such as tomatoes, kiwi fruits and avocados can be placed on a sunny window sill to help them ripen. This also brings out the flavour and encourages their natural juices to flow.

Most fresh vegetables are best stored in the refrigerator. Salad crops, including lettuces, rocket (arugula) and spinach, should be eaten within a few days of purchase. Root vegetables should be left unwashed, as the soil or mud coating helps to keep them fresh. Moisture is retained within the root or tuber, so unwashed carrots, turnips and potatoes keep for much longer than the shiny, scrubbed vegetables that look so pretty but perish so much quicker.

Right: Making flavourful juices from fresh fruit and vegetables is easy and delicious, as in this power booster mix of apple, carrot and beetroot (at back). Blend cucumber, tomatoes, garlic and lemon juice for an energizing summer drink (at front).

Cooking Organic Fruit and Vegetables

Cooking fruit reduces valuable vitamins and minerals, so, if you can, eat it raw. Over-cooking vegetables depletes their nutritional value, destroys their texture, impairs their flavour and spoils their natural colour. It is always advisable to steam vegetables rather than boil them. Boiling vegetables destroys up to half their nutrients, although this figure can be reduced if the vegetables are cooked whole and sliced afterwards. Better still, serve vegetables raw. They will contain many more enzymes than if cooked. Enzymes help us to digest the micronutrients in fresh produce, so, apart from potatoes, aim to cook for as short a time as possible.

Juicing

If you need to use up a stock of fruit or vegetables quickly, simply juice them. This is the most direct way of accessing the nutrients. Any vegetables can be mixed together satisfactorily, but apples are the only fruit that work well with vegetables. By the same token, any combination of fruit can be juiced, but if you want to add a vegetable, make it a carrot. Following these rules ensures that juices do not curdle and are refreshing, delicious and nutritious.

Preserving

For added variety during the winter months, you can preserve organic fruit. Marmalades and jams are easy to make. Drying slices of fruit, such as apples, by baking them overnight in the oven on a very low heat maintains much of the nutritional value while concentrating the taste. It is important to use organic fruit when preserving, as the peel is included. All kinds of organic dried fruit can be bought, from apricots to bananas and mangoes. Non-organic dried fruits are generally treated with sulphur, fungicides and mineral oils, whereas organic varieties are preserved naturally.

Left: Pickling is a great way to preserve extra stocks of all sorts of vegetables, including garlic, small onions and shallots.

ALLIUMS

This family of plants includes onions, leeks, chives and garlic, all of which owe their characteristic odour and flavour to a compound called allicin. Organic alliums contain more allicin than their non-organic counterparts, so have stronger flavours and more health benefits. Organic onions are sweeter, and organic garlic is more pungent. Unfortunately, allicin is also the constituent in alliums that makes us cry, so organic onions should be chopped at arm's length – or by someone else!

Alliums help to lower cholesterol. They also have antibacterial qualities and can help to relieve asthma, bronchitis and other sinus and chest ailments. The cycloallin they contain is an anticoagulant, which thins the blood and helps to protect the heart. Alliums also have anti-fungal properties; the juice can be rubbed on to the skin to relieve fungal infections. Garlic is the most powerful healer of the alliums and has been praised for its medicinal powers for hundreds of years, but all members of the family contain some allicin, so they all have beneficial qualities.

All alliums should be stored in a cool place. It is important to keep them dry or they will begin to sprout. Organic alliums keep just as well as non-organic ones. The wide variety of onions can be enjoyed raw or cooked and, with garlic, add flavour to many savoury dishes.

Below: Red onions have been shown to cut cholesterol radically.

Above: A bunch of baby leeks is a bonus in the autumn organic vegetable box.

Above: Bulb spring onions (scallions) are at their most nutritious when they are raw.

Onions

These are indispensable in the organic kitchen and form the basis of innumerable savoury dishes, including salads, stews, soups and gravies. There are many varieties, including big Spanish onions and small, sweet red onions. Add onions on the side when making a classic organic cooked breakfast. Not only do they taste delicious with bacon and sausages, but they have been shown to cut cholesterol radically.

Garlic

Although it is the most powerful healer of the allium family, this is not garlic's only attribute. It also has a superb flavour. Both hard- and soft-neck varieties are on sale in the organic market, and there is a wealth of taste and colour to explore. Hard-neck garlic, like Pink Music, has a central woody stem surrounded by five to ten easy-to-peel cloves. It has a richer, more rounded flavour than soft-neck garlic, which is the type you often find twisted together, French fashion, to form plaits or braids. Soft-neck garlic, such as Mother of Pearl, has a spicy flavour. Each bulb contains a seemingly endless amount of increasingly smaller cloves.

This type of garlic can be stored for up to a year, unlike hard-neck garlic, which must be used within six months. Fresh organic garlic is available but it is at its best when dried and cured. When the thin skin is papery dry, the cloves are mature and will burst with flavour. Look for a firm head when buying garlic.

Above: Garlic

Leeks

A bunch of sweet, young leeks is a bonus in the autumn organic vegetable box. They are good enough to eat raw, but also taste great when lightly steamed or sautéed with garlic.

Spring Onions/Scallions and Chives

These vegetables taste delicious, especially when raw, when they are at their most nutritious. Organic growers often sell bunches of thin, young spring onions which make delicious snacks.

TUBERS

Whether you are shopping for potatoes, yacons or Jerusalem artichokes, you'll be spoilt for choice, since there are many more varieties of organic tubers available than the few agrochemical types.

Potatoes

A farmers' market or box scheme will provide opportunities to sample unusual types of organic potatoes. There are huge variations in the size and flavour of potatoes, and colours include yellow, red, pink, purple and black. There are two textures: waxy and floury. Common waxy varieties include new potatoes, Pink Fir Apple and Charlotte. Maris Piper and Estima are floury. Yukon Gold and Alaskan Sweetheart are also good.

All potatoes are a good source of vitamin C and the B group vitamins. Organic potatoes are helpful in supporting the body's natural resistance and keeping energy levels steady. Their peel can safely be eaten, boosting fibre levels, nutrition and flavour.

Waxy potatoes are ideal for frying and steaming, while floury potatoes are better for mashing or creaming. Use floury potatoes in leek and potato soup or for chips (French fries) that are soft in the middle, and waxy new potatoes as a springtime accompaniment for lamb chops. Potatoes should be stored in a dark, cool place that is perfectly dry.

Jerusalem Artichokes

Widely available in the autumn months, these delicious vegetables have an unusual, slightly bitter yet buttery flavour, and are excellent served alone or incorporated into dishes. Their bitterness is due to the presence of a compound called *cynarine*. This is a powerful liver stimulant, so eating Jerusalem artichokes will support liver

Above: *Jerusalem artichokes help detoxify the body.*

action, helping to detoxify the body. Organic Jerusalem artichokes also help to alleviate rheumatism and arthritis. Try Jerusalem artichokes lightly steamed with fish, or mashed with potatoes and swedes (rutabagas).

Sweet Potatoes

When cooked, sweet potatoes become sticky and soft with a gorgeous, smooth taste. Organic varieties are particularly sweet and are an excellent source of vitamins, including vitamins C, E and betacarotene, which helps to prevent cancer. They encourage eye and skin health, too. Because organic sweet potatoes are free of fungicides, they can be scrubbed and cooked whole for a wonderfully caramelized alternative to the ubiquitous baked potato. They are also good when steamed and mashed in the same way as regular potatoes.

Yacon Tubers

Almost all yacon tubers are organic. A staple food of the people of the Andes, they can be savoured cooked or raw. They are a good source of complex carbohydrates, with lots of vitamins and minerals. Their crunchy flesh is sweet and juicy like that of a water chestnut or jicama. Try them sliced or grated in leaf or rice salads. When steamed or roasted, the yacon becomes even sweeter. Yacons are not widely available, but can be found through box schemes and at farmers' markets. Store them in the salad drawer of the refrigerator.

Above: *Sweet potatoes are a good source of vitamins, including vitamins C, E and betacarotene.*

Below: *Organic farmers produce many varieties of white and red potatoes.*

ROOTS

The roots are a plant's powerhouse, and root vegetables provide us with a delicious way of tapping into this energy store. Organic root vegetables are often more knobbly and curly than agrochemically grown root vegetables. They deliver more nutrition and flavour than their more uniform counterparts, as well as being more individual in appearance.

All root vegetables should be stored unwashed. As with tubers, a layer of soil helps to seal moisture and nutrients into the roots.

Below: Swedes (rutabaga) contain vitamins A and C.

Carrots

Organically grown carrots are extremely high in betacarotenes, giving them a rich orange colour. Celebrate this with a sweet Middle Eastern salad. Grate four small carrots and mix with the juice of one orange, a few sesame seeds and 5ml/ 1 tsp honey. Alternatively, simply steam lightly or add to stews and stir-fries.

Below: Turnips are credited with soothing aching joints.

Parsnips

Organic parsnips are fragrant and intense. When roasted, they caramelize more successfully than non-organic ones because they are sweeter. Their flavour concentrates and the texture becomes chewy, with a crunch at the tip.

Swedes/Rutabaga and Turnips

There is nothing more comforting on a cold winter night than mashed swede with a little butter and seasoning. Organic turnips have a subtle flavour, underpinned with a bitter edge that people love or hate. They are delicious lightly steamed and served as a side dish for fish. Turnips deliver calcium and potassium and are credited with soothing aching joints.

Beetroot/Beets

Organic beetroot comes in an amazing variety of types. From yellow mangels to the Italian bull's-eye beet, these are the most colourful root vegetables. Young beetroot tastes very good when it is raw and grated. Alternatively, roast them with a medley of other root vegetables.

Left: Radishes are a good source of anti-cancer phytochemicals.

Radishes

When grown organically, radishes are very hot and spicy. They also have more concentrated amounts of anti-cancer phytochemicals. Traditionally, radishes are eaten to stimulate the gall bladder to manufacture digestive juices. The many varieties range from Japanese daikon to the classic red cherry belle. As with all root vegetables, any sign of springiness indicates that a radish is not fresh. Radishes are delicious sliced raw in salads, especially with watercress or rocket (arugula), and are also good in stir-fries.

MAKING A BASIC VEGETABLE STOCK

Homemade stock is a healthier option than the store-bought version and is easy to make. It can be stored in the refrigerator for up to four days. Alternatively, prepare it in large quantities and freeze.

INGREDIENTS
15ml/1 tbsp olive oil
1 potato, chopped
1 carrot, chopped
1 onion, chopped
1 celery stalk, chopped
2 garlic cloves, peeled
1 sprig thyme
1 bay leaf
a few stalks of parsley
600ml/1 pint/2½ cups water
salt and freshly ground pepper

1 Heat the oil in a large pan. Add the vegetables and cook, covered, for 10 minutes, or until softened, stirring occasionally. Stir in the garlic and herbs.

2 Pour the water into the pan, bring to the boil, and simmer, partially covered, for 40 minutes. Strain, season with salt and pepper, and use as required.

VEGETABLE FRUITS

Tomatoes, aubergines (eggplant), (bell) peppers and chillies are treated as vegetables in cooking but classified botanically as fruit.

Tomatoes

There is simply no comparison between the flavour of a freshly picked organic tomato that has been allowed to ripen naturally and the taste of an artificially ripened tomato. Organic growers select the sweetest, tastiest varieties, and whether you buy tiny cherry tomatoes or big beefsteaks, you won't be disappointed.

In terms of nutrition, tomatoes contain a beneficial carotenoid called lycopene. This important micro-nutrient helps to protect the body from cancer, especially cancers of the gastrointestinal tract, breast, cervix and prostate. Lycopene is present in the fresh fruit and is released from the skin when fresh tomatoes are cooked. This means that levels of lycopene are even higher in canned or processed products, such as tomato purée (paste), canned tomatoes, ketchup and pasteurized tomato juice, than they are in fresh tomatoes. However, fresh tomatoes are

Left: Chadwick tomatoes are sweet and juicy.

higher in vitamin C, which is destroyed in cooking. It is absolutely essential to buy organic tomato products since almost all non-organic prepared tomato products contain GMO tomatoes.

Chillies

Fresh chillies come in a wide variety of shapes, sizes and colours, with flavours ranging from mild and fruity to intensely fiery. Organic growers like to experiment with the rarer varieties, so you may find unusual types at a farmers' market. More than 200 different types of chilli are available and they now form an integral part of very many cuisines, including Indian, Thai, Mexican, South American and African.

Right: Serrano chillies contain capsaicin, a phytochemical that is essential for heart health.

CHILLI BOOST

For an instant uplift, sprinkle some organic crushed chilli on your food. The chilli will stimulate the release of endorphins, which are the body's "feel-good" chemicals.

Handle chilli peppers with care, as they can irritate the skin and eyes. Wear gloves when preparing chillies.

Chillies are the concentrated relations of sweet peppers, and there are wonderful stories concerning their heart-strengthening abilities. They also have antibacterial properties and help respiration and chest complaints.

Like peppers, chillies contain *capsaicin*. In chillies, however, it is concentrated, and accounts for their heat. Handle them with care, as the *capsaicin* can damage sensitive skin, especially around the lips and eyes. The hottest part of a chilli is the white membrane that connects the seeds to the flesh. Removing this membrane and the seeds removes most of the heat. The heat can also be moderated and the sweetness released if chillies are roasted or grilled (broiled) until charred, and then peeled in the same way as peppers. Chillies prepared in this way freeze well.

Above: Naturally ripened organic tomatoes contain a beneficial carotenoid called lycopene, which helps protect the body from cancer.

Left: *Organic aubergines are meaty and delicious.*

Aubergines

Organic aubergines are both meaty and delicious. They come in a range of beautiful varieties, from the pretty dappled pink Listada de Gandia to the creamy White Sword. The phytochemical that gives aubergines their bitter flavour helps to prevent and cure the common cold. If you prefer a less bitter taste, slice each vegetable and sprinkle it with salt. Leave for about an hour and the salt will leach out the bitterness, then rinse thoroughly and pat dry before cooking. This also prevents the absorption of excessive oil when frying.

A great way to release the sweetness of aubergines is to bake them. Simply put them, on a baking sheet, in an oven preheated to 180°C/350°F/Gas 4. Cook for about 30 minutes or until tender, then peel the skin from the flesh, chop them and serve drizzled with olive oil, tahini and lemon juice. This popular dish is known as baba ganoush. Aubergines are also delicious roasted, griddled and puréed into garlic-laden dips.

Peppers/Bell Peppers

Agrochemical peppers are often grown hydroponically, which is why they tend to taste inferior to organic ones. Organic peppers are full of vitamin C as well as containing the phytochemical capsaicin that is great for heart health. Green peppers are fully developed but less ripe than other examples, which can make them hard to digest. They have refreshing juicy flesh with a crisp texture. In addition to being more mature, orange, red and purple peppers have sweeter flesh and are more digestible than less ripe green peppers. Roasting or chargrilling peppers enhances their sweetness. Peppers are also delicious when they are served stuffed, sliced into salads or steamed.

Below: *Sweet (bell) peppers are members of the capsicum family. The very best organic peppers are firm and glossy with unblemished skins.*

PEELING (BELL) PEPPERS

1 Roast the peppers under a hot grill (broiler) for 12–15 minutes, turning regularly, until the skin chars.

2 Alternatively, place on a baking sheet and roast in an oven preheated to 200°C/400°F/Gas 6 for 20–30 minutes, until the skin blackens and blisters.

3 Put the peppers in a plastic bag and leave until cool. The steam will encourage the skin to come away from the flesh easily.

4 Peel away the skin, then slice in half. Remove the core and scrape out any remaining seeds. Slice or chop according to your recipe.

MUSHROOMS

Non-organic mushrooms are subjected to vast amounts of chemicals, on the crop itself and to sterilize the straw on which they grow. Fungicides and insecticides are sprayed over them and their growing sheds are regularly bleached. Organic mushrooms have no such hazards. They are also much tastier than most non-organic varieties, whether simply sliced raw in a salad or fried with tamari or soy sauce.

Most organic mushrooms do not contain a wealth of nutrients, but are a useful source of B vitamins, potassium, iron and niacin. Organic shiitake mushrooms, however, are fantastic for the immune system, and have been prized for centuries in Japan for their medicinal properties. They are also a good source of phytochemicals and other nutrients. Dried shiitake mushrooms are readily available in organic stores.

Button (white), cap and flat mushrooms are the most common cultivated variety of mushrooms. They are all one type of mushroom in various stages of maturity, from small button mushrooms, through cap mushrooms to the largest, strongest-flavoured flat mushrooms. Flat mushrooms are good grilled (broiled) or baked on their own or with stuffing.

Left: Fresh and dried shiitake mushrooms are fantastic for the immune system.

Chestnut (cremini) mushrooms look similar to button mushrooms but have brown caps and a nutty flavour. Field (portabello) mushrooms are wild and have intense, rich flavour, which makes them ideal for grilling and stuffing. Chanterelles are a pretty yellow colour, with a funnel-shape and a fragrant but delicate flavour. Available dried as well as fresh, they are delicious sautéed, baked or added to sauces.

Store fresh organic mushrooms in paper bags in the refrigerator, and use within a few days of purchase. When you are ready to eat them, wipe the mushrooms gently with damp kitchen paper and trim the stems. Wild mushrooms often harbour grit and dirt and may need to be rinsed briefly under cold running water but they must be dried thoroughly. Never soak fresh mushrooms or they will become soggy.

PREPARING DRIED SHIITAKE MUSHROOMS

Dried shiitake mushrooms are a useful store-cupboard stand-by. Before they can be used in cooking, however, they must be rehydrated.

1 Quickly wash off any dirt under cold running water, then soak dried shiitake mushrooms in tepid water for about 2–3 hours, or overnight. If you are short of time, soak for at least 45 minutes before cooking.

2 Remove the shiitake from the soaking water, and gently squeeze out any excess water. With your fingers or a knife, trim off the stem and then slice or chop the caps to use in cooking. Add the stems to soups or stock. Don't discard the soaking liquid; rather drain it through muslin (cheesecloth), then use it in soups or stews or for simmering vegetables.

Left: This mixed selection of organic mushrooms is a useful source of B vitamins, iron, potassium and niacin.

PEAS, BEANS and CORN

These popular organic vegetables can be bought frozen as well as fresh so you can enjoy them all year round. They are frozen within hours of being picked and so are still high in nutritional value.

Left: Organic corn cobs have sweet kernels.

Peas and Beans

Organic farmers often rely on legume crops to keep their fields fertile, so there is usually an abundant and varied supply of peas and beans, from sweet mangetouts (snow peas) to meaty broad (fava) beans. Early summer brings the first garden peas, so sweet and tender that you can eat them raw, straight from the pod. This season is short, but other delights lie ahead. Crisp French (green) beans, sugar snaps and runner beans soon appear on organic market stalls.

Shelled peas are best eaten lightly steamed or added to sauces and stews in the last few minutes of cooking. Mangetouts and beans can be sliced raw into salads, stir-fried or lightly steamed as a side dish. Store fresh peas and beans in the salad compartment of the refrigerator and use them within a week to ensure the best taste.

Corn

Organic corn cobs are often smaller and paler than the agrochemical equivalent, but the kernels are beautifully tender and sweet. Corn cobs are best eaten soon after picking, before their natural sugars start to convert into starch, the kernels begin to toughen and their flavour fades. Remove the green outer leaves and cook whole or slice off the kernels with a sharp knife. Baby corn can be eaten raw, and are also good in stir-fries. One delicious way to serve corn on the cob is to fry it whole in hot olive oil for just a few minutes. The heat will be just enough to release the natural sweetness and caramelize the exterior.

Left: Organic mangetouts and sugar snap peas have a fresh flavour.

Eda-mame

These are fresh soya beans. They are widely available in Japan and in many parts of the USA. Eda-mame deliver a complete balance of protein and phytochemicals that are good for maintaining healthy hormone levels.

PREPARING EDA-MAME

This is a good way to appreciate young soya beans in the pod.

1 Separate the pods from the stalks, if they are still attached, and trim off the stem end. Sprinkle the pods generously with salt and rub the salt into the bean pods with your hands. Leave for 15 minutes.

2 Boil plenty of water in a large pan, then add the beans and boil over a high heat for 7–10 minutes, or until the beans are tender but still crunchy. Drain immediately and refresh briefly under running water.

3 Serve hot or cold in a basket or a bowl with drinks. To eat, squeeze the pods with your teeth to push out the beans into your mouth.

SEA VEGETABLES

Also known as seaweeds, these amazing vegetables, with unusual, tangy flavours and exotic colours, provide our strongest natural source of minerals and trace elements. Nori, wakame and hijiki are the richest sources of minerals. Nori is also the best source of protein.

Although Japan and China are the countries best known for their use of sea vegetables, seaweeds have been collected all over the world for centuries.

One interesting property of seaweeds is their ability to detoxify the body thanks to the alginic acid they contain. When we ingest this substance, it binds with heavy metals in our intestines and allows them to be released, cleansing the body. Nori, laver, dulse, kombu, wakame and arame are all types of seaweeds with these detoxifying properties.

Fresh seaweed requires little preparation. Having been gathered in clean and unpolluted water, it needs to be rinsed in fresh water before being dried in the sun or in an oven on a very low heat. It can also be chopped and frozen.

Most seaweeds are only available dried. Once reconstituted they can be used as substitutes for fresh green vegetables, toasted and crumbled over soups, salads or stir-fries, or used in sushi. Unopened packets of dried sea vegetables keep well for several months if stored in a cool place. Canned organic seaweeds often taste stronger than the dried versions.

Nori

The traditional sushi wrap, nori is one sea vegetable that does not require soaking. It comes in purple-black sheets which, when toasted for use as a garnish, turn translucent green.

Above: Dried and cut wakame can be used in stews and salads.

Below: Toasted nori sheets add crunch when used as a garnish.

TOASTING NORI
This brings out the flavour and makes nori crispy. Take care not to scorch the nori sheets – or your fingers.

1 Hold a sheet of nori with a pair of tongs about 5cm/2in above a gas burner for about 1 minute, moving it around so it toasts evenly and turns bright green and crisp.

2 Leave the nori to cool for a few moments. Crumble between your fingers and sprinkle over soups, salads or stir-fries, or use in sushi.

Wakame
A dark-coloured seaweed with a delicate flavour, wakame adds body to stews and can also be used in salads. A small strip, cooked with beans and pulses, will help to soften them. Prepare it in the same way as arame.

Kombu
A strongly flavoured seaweed with flat fronds, kombu, or kelp as it is also known, is used in slowly cooked dishes. It is an essential ingredient in the Japanese stock, dashi.

PREPARING DRIED HIJIKI

Soaking and cooking times vary depending on how the hijiki is to be used.

1 Rinse the hijiki in a strainer under cold, running water, then place in a bowl and cover with tepid water. Leave to soak for 15 minutes – it will expand to several times its dried volume. Drain and place in a pan.

2 Add fresh water to cover the hijiki and bring to the boil. Simmer for about 20 minutes until tender.

Above: Hijiki requires longer cooking than most sea vegetables.

Below: Laver is high in minerals and vitamins.

Arame

Mild-tasting arame is a good sea vegetable to try if you haven't tasted these vegetables before. It must be soaked in warm water for 20 minutes before using in salads or stir-fries, but can be added straight from the packet to slow-cooked noodle dishes and soups.

Hijiki

This twiggy, black sea vegetable looks similar to arame but is thicker and has a stronger flavour. It requires longer cooking than most sea vegetables.

Laver

Commonly found around the shores of Britain, laver is used in regional dishes such as Welsh laverbread, where it is combined with oatmeal. It can be added to sauces and stuffings.

Dulse

A purple-red sea vegetable, dulse has a chewy texture and spicy flavour when cooked. It can be added to salads. In Wales, Ireland, North America and Canada, dulse is gathered in summer and sold in health food stores and fish markets. It is great in noodle dishes and soups or toasted and crumbled for a nourishing garnish.

Right: Dulse has a spicy flavour.

Agar-agar

A setting agent, derived from a type of seaweed called "rock flower vegetable" in China, agar-agar is an ideal vegetarian alternative to gelatine. Available in strips or as powder, it can be used to make excellent sweet or savoury jellies.

HERBS and EDIBLE FLOWERS

Fresh and dried herbs have been prized by cooks for centuries for their ability to enhance the flavour of any ingredient they accompany and enliven even the simplest meal. It is a bonus that many herbs have remarkable healing qualities.

Typically, organic herbs have stronger flavours than non-organic ones because they have a higher concentration of phytochemicals. These active components are the main source of a herbal plant's flavour and health-promoting properties. Non-organic herbs all have the medicinal and taste benefits of organic herbs, but often contain much smaller amounts of the essential oils vital for these purposes. Since it is rare for cooks to wash fresh herbs thoroughly before use, pesticide residues on non-organic herbs can be inadvertently included in a meal. Dried non-organic herbs carry the same risk.

Another big plus when buying herbs from organic growers is the sheer variety and number of plants on offer, including unusual and heirloom varieties such as apple mint, purple basil and Chinese chives. By shopping from organic growers direct, or sourcing organic seeds, the organic cook has access to a much broader selection of flavours.

Growing Herbs

It is essential to use fresh herbs before they start to wilt, and the best way to guarantee freshness is to grow your own herbs in pots or in a window box. Good herbs that grow all year round are parsley, thyme, chives, marjoram, winter savory, sorrel and tarragon. These perennials are quite difficult to grow from seed, so they are best bought as young plants.

Annual herbs such as mint or basil can be grown from seeds sown from late March onwards. They should be sown in seed compost in shallow trays and transferred to bigger containers after about a month. Herbs should always be grown outside, and stone or terracotta pots are best. Traditional herb pots not only look attractive, with their little pockets on the sides, but also work well. All herbs need to be kept under cover on the very coldest nights of winter, but can otherwise stay outside on a window sill or balcony, or in the garden.

Right: Basil is said to have a calming effect on the stomach, easing constipation, sickness and cramps, and aiding digestion.

MAKING BOUQUET GARNI
Tie herbs in a bundle, or bouquet garni, when you want the flavour but not the herbs themselves in a dish.

1 With a long piece of string, tie together a few parsley stalks, a sprig of thyme and a bay leaf, or your own choice of herbs. Add a piece of celery stick to flavour poultry dishes, a spring of rosemary for lamb, or a piece of fennel or leek for fish dishes.

2 Dried or chopped herbs can be bundled together in a small muslin (cheesecloth) bag. Break or tear the herbs into small pieces and place in the centre of a 10–13cm/4–5in square of clean muslin. Bring the edges of the muslin up over the herbs and tie firmly into a bag with a length of string. Make muslin bundles in batches so that they are readily at hand for cooking.

3 Tie one end of the string to the pan handle or leave it hanging over the edge of the casserole to make it easy to remove and discard the herbs before serving the dish.

I Peel the ap
and slice the f
salted water f
prevent discol

2 Thread the
length of strir
ceiling or susp
until they are

3 Alternative
a single layer
baking sheet,
are not touch
set to 70°C/I
several hours

Culinary Combinations

The reason why particular herbs are traditionally added to certain dishes has something to do with complementary flavours, but there are other practical considerations, too. The classic combination of fried lamb's liver with sage not only tastes superb, but the sage helps the body to digest the meat. Organic rosemary contains powerful essential oils that stimulate the digestive system to make extra bile. This makes it the perfect partner for lamb and chicken dishes. Bay leaves added to bolognese sauce aid the digestion of a pasta meal, and the mint tea that customarily concludes the meal in many countries helps to counter indigestion. It also sweetens the breath and because it is a mild stimulant, the diner is less likely to fall asleep on a full stomach.

Preparing Leafy Herbs

Organic herbs do not need to be washed, but different herbs should be prepared in different ways. Such woody-stemmed herbs as sage and thyme need their leaves removed from the stems before adding to dishes. Large leaves can be picked off with the fingers. For small leaves, hold a sprig of herb at the tip and strip off the leaves with a fork.

Leafy herbs, including parsley, can simply be chopped once any coarse stalks have been removed. Cutting herbs with a knife or scissors damages the essential oils from the plant, making them taste more bitter. Try tearing the delicate leaves and stems to encourage a sweeter flavour.

Lightly crushing, or bruising, whole leaves or sprigs of herbs with a mortar and pestle helps to release their flavour into dishes that are cooked quickly.

Use herbs as soon as possible after picking. If you must store them briefly, do so in the refrigerator, wrapped in foil or paper, or chop and freeze them.

Herb Oils

Flavoured oils are delicious for cooking chicken and fish or drizzling over roasted vegetables. Strongly flavoured herbs such as thyme, bay, basil, rosemary, marjoram and tarragon are best suited to flavouring oils. Push several sprigs into a clean, empty bottle. Fill with light olive or sunflower oil and store in a cool place for two weeks. Then strain through muslin into clean bottles. Herb oils will keep for three to six months.

Edible Flowers

Whole flowers or individual petals can enhance savoury and sweet dishes with their delicate flavours. The visual appeal of adding whole flowers or individual petals to a recipe is immediate and wonderful. Flowers from plants with other culinary uses usually taste like a milder version of that plant.

Cooking with organic flowers rather than non-organic flowers is hugely preferably because they are more likely to be strongly scented and, therefore, strongly flavoured. They are available in a fantastic range of species.

Cut deep pink carnation petals from the bitter base of each flower and soak in white wine for half an hour.

Left: Chives and bay leaves add flavour to any organic meal.

Above: Rosemary and sage

Pour the mixture over a fruit salad. Raw sunflower petals add vibrancy to stir-fries. Deep blue cornflowers and bright orange calendula petals transform a green salad, and nasturtiums add peppery bite. Passion flowers, fuchsias, pansies and violas are a dramatic garnish for cakes. Violet and rose petals are traditionally used throughout Europe candied as cake decorations. Lavender and rose waters are made by steeping the flowers in hot water until it cools, then straining the mixture. In Eastern Europe and the Middle East, dried rose petals and rose water are mixed into such dishes as couscous and tagines.

APP

SUMMER FRUITS

Few sight
more plea
than an o
of mature
organic a
and pear
summer. I
and pink
grass like
dart betw
The fruits
they will
fragrance
spent clin
Later, in a
insects on
with a wi
The fruit
are delici
vitamins,

Agroc
grown in
from the
Single spe
rows, ove
systemati

The delicate juicy sweetness of organic summer fruits is one of the greatest joys of the summer months. Like all fruit, these are generally best when home-grown and in season.

Cherries and Plums

From the palest of yellow varieties to the dark-red morellos, cherries are the prettiest of fruits. Plums are just as varied, from tiny greengages to regal Victorias. Agrochemical plums and cherries are treated with differing levels of respect by the farmers who grow them, from widespread use of agrochemicals

Above: *Cherries are high in phytochemicals.*

Above:
*Elegant Lady
peaches*

Above: *Organic plums contain malic acid and betacarotene, which protect against heart disease.*

in some countries to near abstinence in the UK's cherry industry. Unless you can be certain that no agrochemicals have been used, it is safer to choose organic plums and cherries to eat unpeeled. Both plums and cherries are a good source of phytochemicals and may help to prevent cancer and relieve rheumatism and arthritis. Plums contain malic acid and betacarotene, so they can provide protection against heart disease and circulatory disorders. Plums also relieve fluid retention and are good for digestion. Plums can be sweet and juicy or slightly tart; the latter are best cooked in pies and cakes or made into a jam.

Sweet plums can be eaten as they are but are also good in fruit salads and fruit pies. There are also two types of cherries: sweet and sour. Some, such as the popular Bing, are best eaten raw, while others, such as Morello, are best cooked.

Below: *Victoria plums may help relieve rheumatism and arthritis.*

Peaches, Nectarines and Apricots

Organic peaches, nectarines and apricots tend to be smaller and more intensely coloured than non-organic fruit, and are much sweeter and tastier. They help to regulate the system and ease constipation. Ripe peaches and apricots should be stored in the refrigerator but brought to room temperature before eating.

STONING A PEACH

I Slice through the seam line all around the peach.

2 Twist the two halves in opposite directions to separate them.

3 Lever out the stone with a knife.

BERRIES and CURRANTS

Among the most popular of all fruits are berries and currants, with their glowing colours and sweet, scented juices. Strawberries, raspberries, currants of all colours, cranberries, blackberries and blueberries are just some of the delights that are sold throughout the summer. These are strictly seasonal crops. Buy them out of season and they will be inferior in terms of taste, texture and nutrition and they will almost certainly have been brought great distances by air.

Berries are delicate fruit. Washing them can spoil their texture and flavour. This is just one of the reasons why it is best to buy organic. It is perfectly safe to pop an organic berry into your mouth, whereas the agrochemical fruit will have been heavily sprayed with herbicides, fungicides, insecticides and slug deterrents. Organic berries are smaller and sweeter than non-organic ones.

Strawberries
From organic growers, strawberries are naturally sweet and delicious. Their flavour is concentrated in smaller, less watery fruit. As with all berries and grapes, they are high in vitamin C. Strawberries are also rich in soluble fibre and beta-carotene and contain phytochemicals that help to ease arthritis.

Below: Organic strawberries are naturally firm and delicious.

Above: Organic blueberries are strong cancer-preventing berries.

Above: Cranberries are a good source of vitamins A and C and potassium.

Blackberries
These high-fibre berries contain a wealth of minerals including iron, magnesium and calcium. They are rich in the bioflavonoids, which act as antioxidants, inhibiting the growth of cancer cells and protecting against cell damage by carcinogens.

Raspberries
These soft and fragrant berries are effective in removing toxins from the body. To make an uncooked purée or coulis, process some raspberries in a food processor or blender until smooth. Sweeten with maple syrup to taste and add a splash of lemon juice to bring out the flavour. For a smooth purée press through a nylon strainer. Store raspberries in the refrigerator for up to two days.

Right: Raspberries are high in vitamin C.

Blueberries
These are exciting considerable interest in terms of cancer research, being rich in anthocyanidins, the phytochemicals that give them their blue colour. The consensus is that they can help prevent cancer.

Cranberries
An excellent source of vitamin C, cranberries also provide potassium and vitamin A. Cranberry juice is effective in treating such infections of the urinary tract as cystitis.

Redcurrants
These pretty, delicate berries are rich in antioxidants, carotene and vitamins A and C.

Below: Redcurrants

Below: Blackberries

GRAPES, MELONS and FIGS

Some of the first fruits ever cultivated, grapes, melons and figs are now available in an enormous range of shapes, colours and sizes. They are excellent sources of essential nutrients.

Grapes

There are hundreds of different kinds of organic grapes available, from the largest black sweet varieties through to tiny seedless white ones. Wine grapes are often incredibly fragrant and remarkably differing in taste, texture, size, consistency and acidity. Semillon grapes are a classic variety from South West France, now grown from Australia to California. They have a delightful honey-like taste. Sauvignon grapes have herbal and melon flavours, with a citrus fruit edge. Friulian grapes are floral and crisply acidic, whereas Marsanne grapes are relatively low in acidity with a smooth nutty tone to their flavour.

Right: Delicious raw, organic figs can also be poached or baked.

Below: Grapes are high in vitamin C and carbohydrates.

Organic grapes are naturally high in antioxidants. They provide the perfect pick-up for convalescents, being a good source of carbohydrates and vitamin C. Grapes are easy to eat and taste delicious. Eat them at any time except after a big meal, as they tend to ferment and upset the stomach if it is full. They are best eaten straight off the bunch, or chopped into fruit salads, and taste excellent in fresh green salads.

Figs

The wonderful squashy texture of organic figs's flesh is the perfect foil for their crispy seeds, and the delicate fruit has a fantastically sweet and toffee-like flavour. Figs can be eaten raw but are also delicious poached or baked. These fruits are a great cure for constipation and, since they are high in iron, figs can help protect the body against anaemia.

Melons

There are two kinds of melons – musk melons and watermelons. Musk melons include the honeydew and Israeli HaOgen varieties. Their flesh is typically sweet and peach coloured. Watermelons include the classic pink-fleshed and deep-green-skinned varieties as well as rare paler versions such as the Early Moonbeam with its yellow flesh and striped green skin.

Agrochemically grown melons are sprayed with particularly noxious chemicals, including lindane and paraquat. The danger of ingesting these chemicals through a melon's skin is low, as only the inside flesh is eaten. However, if a melon plant is sprayed with pesticides and then watered, it is possible that some of the agrochemical will be diluted in the water. Melons are storehouses of the water used to irrigate them. Organic melons are refreshing and cleansing, easing fluid retention and urinary problems. Try serving them cubed on sticks or simply serve a crescent in its skin, decorated with small summer fruits. Melons are also delicious in sweet and savoury salads.

Left: Organic watermelons are filled with the unpolluted water used to irrigate them.

CITRUS FRUITS

Native to every warm to tropical country, citrus fruits are the most ubiquitous of tropical fruits and are enjoyed throughout the globe, from northern Europe to the southern tip of Chile. Oranges, grapefruit, lemons, limes, pomelos, tangerines, satsumas, kumquats and mandarins are all grown organically. They should be strongly favoured over cheaper agrochemical alternatives.

Agrochemical citrus fruits are heavily treated with a huge range of powerful agrochemical toxins. Over one hundred different agrochemicals are permitted for use on citrus orchards in the USA, with a potentially higher and more dangerous toxic cocktail applied to citrus crops in the developing world. Organic citrus fruits are not dyed, whereas many agrochemically grown ones are injected with artificial colourings.

All of the members of the organic citrus family benefit from being grown as nature intended. Vitamin and mineral levels are boosted and the fruits are packed with bioflavonoids. The benefits of wax-free citrus peel are obvious to jam makers, with organic marmalade being the best choice by far. All citrus fruits are great for preventing or treating colds and sore throats and generally raising immunity.

Lemons

Smaller and more irregularly shaped than agrochemical lemons, organic lemons are juicy and tart. Although all citrus fruits contain citric acid, lemons have an amazing property that means they work as an alkaline food. When the human body digests lemon juice, a by-product is potassium carbonate. This salt actually neutralizes the digestive system, creating a beneficial balance.

In the kitchen, lemons have limitless uses. From soups to sorbets, there is scarcely a dish that does not benefit from a squeeze of lemon juice or a sprinkling of grated rind. When lemon juice is squirted over cooked meats, fish and vegetables, the lemon juice caramelizes to crisp the main ingredient.

Organic lemons are not dyed and they are sometimes greener than agrochemical ones. Ripe lemons will yield to the touch when you squeeze them lightly. Rolling a lemon firmly over a work surface or in the palms of your hands will help you extract the maximum amount of juice.

Unwaxed, organic lemon rind adds an understated warmth to the dish and contributes bacteria-fighting limonine oils. The juice itself is packed with vitamin C and numerous phytochemicals, supporting the development of general health, and will help the body to build a strong immune system.

Below: Organic oranges

Oranges and Grapefruit

Organic citrus fruits have more vitality – grapefruits are tarter and oranges are rounder in flavour. Like many other agrochemical citrus crops, non-organic oranges and grapefruit are routinely coated with anti-fungal waxes that would contaminate any dishes prepared with citrus rind or peel. If the skin of the fruit is matt, not shiny, this is evidence that it has not been waxed. Both fruits are high in vitamin C and grapefruits offer valuable support for gum health. Try squeezing grapefruit juice into a fruit cocktail to add zest, or simply halve the fruit and eat it with a spoon.

Below: Unwaxed organic lemons

Limes

Once considered an exotic fruit, limes are now a part of every modern cook's kitchen. The juice has a sharper flavour than that of lemons, so use less juice if you substitute limes for lemons in a recipe. Limes are an essential part of organic holistic cancer treatment.

Left: Organic limes

TROPICAL FRUITS

Organic kiwi fruits, pineapples, papaya and mangoes are abundant sources of vitamin C. All of these fruits tend to be smaller than their non-organic equivalents, with denser and sweeter flesh. They also have higher levels of micronutrients, which result in rounded, more intense flavours.

Left: Kiwi fruit contain as much fibre as pears.

Most tropical fruits are naturally high in sugar, so they should be picked and eaten as soon as they are ripe. As they are often transported vast distances, this creates a temptation for agrochemical growers to pick under-ripe fruit for shipment. Organic farmers, however, allow fruit to ripen naturally for longer, which improves the nutritional content and flavour. When fully ripe, organic mangoes, kiwi fruit and papayas all feel slightly soft when squeezed. Organic tropical fruit should be eaten as soon as it is ripe, because it has a relatively short shelf life.

Kiwi Fruits

Packed with potassium, organic kiwi fruits can alleviate depression and fatigue and help control high blood pressure. Kiwis contain similar amounts of vitamin C to lemons, and about the same amount of fibre as pears. Organic kiwi fruits are smaller and furrier than non-organic ones, with darker and less watery flesh.

Papayas

The enzyme papain contained in organic papayas cleanses the digestive tract and aids general immunity and health. Papaya seeds are crunchy and spicy. Try eating them sprinkled on savoury green salads to add bite.

Mangoes

Organic mangoes are rich in vitamin C and carotene and are also reputed to cleanse the blood. To make an exotic tropical fruit salad, cube mangoes, papayas, kiwi fruits and pineapple and drizzle them with some freshly squeezed orange juice and a little maple syrup.

Papayas (above) and mangoes (below) are rich in vitamin C and carotene.

PREPARING A MANGO

I Place the mango narrow side down on a chopping board. Cut off a thick lengthways slice, keeping the knife as close to the stone as possible. Turn the mango round and repeat on the other side. Cut off the flesh adhering to the stone and scoop the flesh from the mango slices.

2 To make a "hedgehog", prepare the mango as above and then score the flesh on each thick slice with criss-cross lines at 1cm/½in intervals, taking care not to cut through the skin.

3 Carefully turn the mango halves inside out and serve.

Left: Bananas are high in dietary fibre and a major source of potassium, which can relieve high blood pressure.

Below: Pineapples have an enzyme called bromelain, which is good for the digestive system.

Bananas

Like kiwi fruits, organic bananas are a major source of potassium. They are also very good for the digestion. It is well known that eating ripe bananas eases constipation, but they are also good for curing diarrhoea. Agrochemical bananas can contain pesticides, so choose organic fruit when feeding children.

Pineapples

Organic pineapples are prized for their high enzyme content. One of these, bromelain, acts as a deep cleanser for the digestive system, improving the uptake of all nutritional compounds. They are also fantastic for the complexion, especially when applied topically.

Dates

Organic dates are a rich source of dietary fibre, potassium and folic acid. Their extremely sweet taste makes dates wonderful to bake with. Add them chopped to fruit cakes and steamed puddings, or eat them whole. They can be given to children instead of sweets (candies), and are a useful food for people needing extra energy, including sportsmen and women, pregnant women and the elderly. Non-organic dates are often soaked in syrups and oils, but you will find that organic dates are naturally sweet.

Left: Organic dates are naturally sweet and high in energy.

DRIED FRUIT

When dried, many of the nutrients in a fruit are concentrated, as are the natural sugars, but, unfortunately, so are pesticide residues. Non-organic dried figs, for instance, not only contain more pesticides weight for weight than fresh figs, but they also contain added fungicides. Organic dried fruit is clearly a better option.

Dried apricots are particularly useful, not only for eating in the hand, but also for baking or in jam. They are a rich source of carotenes and, when eaten in quantity, contain useful quantities of vitamin C. As such they are the staple and only protection from scurvy available to many people in remote mountain communities, such as the Himalayan area of Ladakh. Organic dried apricots have also been credited with helping to reduce high blood pressure, protecting against cancer and supporting clear, naturally beautiful skin.

MEAT, POULTRY and GAME

Meat and poultry that has been farmed organically is the prime choice for cooks whose criteria are good quality, fine taste and texture, and whose concerns include basic levels of animal welfare. Intensively produced meat is almost always bland, watery, fatty and laced with unnatural hormones, antibiotics and drugs. Welfare conditions for the animals that provide non-organic meat are often horrific, from their rearing to slaughter. Although there are some excellent small non-organic meat farms, and free-range meat is better than meat from intensively reared animals and birds, choosing organic meat and poultry is the only option that fully addresses the issues.

Organic meat labelled as such by a recognized certifying body is also the only option if you want to avoid genetically modified organisms, because about 99 per cent of all non-organic meat is produced from animals whose feed contains some GMOs.

Farming Methods
Non-organic, intensively farmed animals and birds are taken away from their mothers within a few days of birth and reared in huge herds and flocks. Most of their lives are spent indoors, and they are fed unnatural dried food pellets laced with growth hormones. Antibiotics are used routinely as a safeguard against the diseases and parasites that flourish in the cramped and stressful conditions in which they are kept. Animals and birds are brought to maturity as quickly as possible, by feeding them growth hormones, which speed up the process.

When intensively farmed livestock are ready for slaughter, they generally travel long distances in cramped lorries to the abattoir. In 2001, the European Union exported about 875,000 tonnes of live cows and beef to the rest of the world. At the same time, about 170,000 tonnes of live cows and beef were imported into Europe from Argentina, Botswana, Poland and Brazil. The growth of intensive meat farms has eradicated small local abattoirs, with huge centralized slaughterhouses replacing them for the processors' convenience.

Animal welfare is at the heart of organic animal husbandry. Animals are allowed to feed more freely and grow naturally, resulting in meat and poultry that tastes very much better.

The absolute freedom of game's wild existence means that it cannot be classified as organic. However, truly wild game from unpolluted countryside areas is an excellent choice for anyone who supports animal welfare and freedom. Farmed game that is organically certified is delicious and sustainable.

Biodynamic farming really comes into its own for meat products. Biodynamic animals live extremely comfortable lives, from birth to the abattoir. Many different kinds of heirloom and rare breed animals are free to mingle under cover or outdoors, in scenes reminiscent of an old-fashioned dream of how an animal farm should be. In the UK, regional species of pig such as the Tamworth porker are reared biodynamically, whereas this breed is almost unheard of on commercial intensive meat farms. While organic farm animals, which are unwell, may be treated with chemical medicines if homeopathy and other

Above: *Animals raised on organic farms enjoy a healthy, stress-free lifestyle.*

complementary treatments do not work, biodynamic animals must be entirely chemical free. Meat is always hung after slaughter, which helps the flavour to develop. While this process occurs with all quality organic and non-organic meats, biodynamic meat is guaranteed to benefit from this traditional treatment.

Buying Organic Meat
Everybody who wants to eat delicious organic meat and poultry is encouraged to experiment with different stores or direct buying schemes. It is convenient to be able to obtain organic meat from the supermarket, but it is worth considering what is on offer at specialist fine organic suppliers and farmers' markets as well as local box schemes.

All organic meat tastes good because the animals are free range and feed on grass. The best organic meat tastes even better, however, because the carcasses are hung in the traditional manner after slaughter. Buying from a local supplier or taking delivery of organic meat from a box scheme will also provide you with cooking tips as part of the service. Another important advantage of buying meat either direct or from a specialist outlet is that the purchaser can often order an old-fashioned cut or ask for meat to be prepared in a particular way.

Organic halal and kosher meat is available in some larger Islamic and Jewish communities through mail order and box schemes. Check local Islamic or Jewish journals or search the Internet for details of a scheme near you.

Biodynamic and organic meats may be more expensive than intensively farmed meat, but this is not necessarily a bad thing. Reducing the quantity of meat we consume is recommended by doctors and nutritionists. When meat becomes an occasional treat, the cost is not so relevant, especially when the quality is first rate. Occasional meat eating is much more in line with man's original diet than daily hamburgers. Enjoyed weekly or fortnightly, organic meat will regain its special place in our diet.

Beef and Veal

Organic beef contains a much better balance of good and bad cholesterol than meat from intensively reared cows. This is because the animals' diet includes a high content of grass, whereas many intensively reared cattle are fed dry food almost exclusively. Some good quality non-organic beef cattle benefit from a free-range, grass-fed existence,

Above: Organic beef rib is a healthier choice.

but buying organic beef ensures this happens.

For a classic roast beef, use either sirloin or fore rib. Back rib and topside (pot roast) are both excellent slow roasted. When grilling (broiling) or frying steaks, use sirloin, rib eye, rump or fillet steaks. Neck or clod has an open, slightly sticky texture, and is good for stews, whereas shin (shank), chuck steak and top rump are best for casseroles where whole slices are needed. Pot roast silverside or brisket cuts, as these need to be cooked slowly over a long period. Flank and thin flank are good for making mince (ground beef) for bolognese sauces and cottage pies. Minced (ground) clod and shin are great for hamburgers and steak tartare because they are virtually fat free. Shin makes a good filling for slow-cooked pies.

If you buy veal make sure that it is organic. It will not be as pale as intensively farmed veal but you will have the satisfaction of knowing that it has come from a calf that has been reared with its mother, rather than being removed when only a few days old, which causes both animals great distress. Veal steaks are best simply pan-fried to seal in their flavour.

Above: Organic lamb is especially tender and full of flavour.

Mutton and Lamb

Most good supermarkets offer organic lamb, but usually only as chops and mince (ground lamb). Organic lamb is tender and full of flavour. The fat is clearly visible and can be removed easily. Organic mutton can be harder to find but many organic butchers stock it. It is invaluable for many authentic dishes, especially stews with an Arabic flavour. Minced mutton or lamb, which comes from shoulder, belly or leg meat, can be used instead of minced beef.

For a classic roast mutton or roast lamb, use leg, shoulder, saddle or rack. If you like your lamb pink, choose saddle or rack of lamb. Grill (broil) or fry leg steaks, loin or chump chops or cutlets. The rarer the meat, the more tender and flavoursome it will be. Lamb and mutton can both be fatty, but the meat can easily be trimmed. Make kebabs from neck fillet (US shoulder or breast) and butterflied or cubed leg. Casserole middle neck or shoulder meat for classic dishes such as navarin of lamb.

Right: Organic pork loin is a popular cut for roasting.

Pork

There are lots of delicious organic pork products available, including traditional home-made sausages, honey roasted hams, gammon and bacon. Most organic and non-organic bacon is cured with saltpetre. Although this helps to preserve the pinkish colour of the meat, there are some concerns about whether this traditional process is entirely healthy. A few specialist organic and biodynamic pork farms now offer fine-quality pork products that do not contain this ingredient. The meat they sell is darker, with a brown rather than red tinge, but it tastes just as delicious. High-quality organic pork sausages are widely available in supermarkets and delicatessens, but as with all organic meat products, traditional organic farmers' markets and delivery services offer an even more extensive range. Look out for pork sausages with apple, sage or forest fruits, as well as preserved salamis and saucissons.

Pork is a tender meat, which is suitable for all forms of cooking. Leg is a popular cut for roasting, as is blade, which can be roasted on the bone or boned and stuffed. For a truly succulent roast, try spare rib. Perhaps the most popular cut for roasting is loin, which provides the best crackling. To achieve this, score the fat deeply, rub in salt and roast the joint dry. When grilling (broiling) pork chops or steaks, it is essential to watch them carefully. They must be cooked through, as underdone pork can cause infection, but they should not be allowed to dry out.

Pork fillet (tenderloin) and schnitzel steaks are the best choice for frying. For braising, choose pork chops, steaks, spare ribs, blade, loin or belly meat. Hand and spring meat is a large cut which can be cubed and cooked in tender pork casseroles and stews.

Above: Organic chilli and pepper salami (left) and hot salami are all available from specialist organic butchers and organic stores.

Poultry

Organic poultry tends to be less fatty than intensively reared equivalents because the birds have more freedom to exercise and are not fed growth hormones. Because it is less fatty the meat benefits from being cooked slowly.

Organic chicken, duck, goose and turkey are easy to obtain, but goose and turkey tend to be more seasonal, their availability linked to festivals such as Christmas, Easter and Thanksgiving. As well as whole birds, poultry portions and breast fillets are available. They may be on the bone or boneless. Buying whole birds and cutting them up is not difficult, however, and provides the perfect opportunity for making homemade stock.

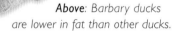

Above: Barbary ducks are lower in fat than other ducks.

Duck and Goose These are fatty birds with dark meat that has plenty of flavour. The fat helps to keep the meat moist during cooking. Goose is nearly always roasted, though the legs may be added to casseroles. Ducks are generally roasted whole or cut up for frying or casseroling.

American Long Island and British Aylesbury ducks have paler, tender meat with a significant proportion of fat and a rich flavour. Barbary and Nantes ducks have slightly less fat. The barbary, a big bird, provides a good proportion of firm breast meat. The Nantes is smaller, more tender and with a delicate flavour.

Unlike other domesticated poultry, geese have defied all attempts to rear them intensively. They are not prolific layers and are one of the few remaining sources of seasonal food. Goose fat is used in traditional cooking across central and Eastern Europe and in Scandinavia.

Chicken and Turkey Organic birds are raised in humane conditions, fed on a natural and (usually) traditional-style diet. They do not have lurid-coloured skin. The skeleton of an organic bird is bigger and stronger, and the legs are longer. When cooked, the flesh is less uniform in colour and texture; the breast meat is paler and the leg darker. Standards and conditions relating to the scheme or terms by which the birds are classified as organic are usually outlined on the packaging.

As well as whole birds, chicken and turkey are available in a wide choice of portions. Look for birds with a clear, soft skin, with no bruises or blemishes. The tougher the skin, the older the bird.

Organic chicken and turkey need to be cooked slower and longer than non-organic poultry to get the best flavour and texture. When roasting, try stuffing the cavity with grains and herbs, or with fresh fruit and spices, for an aromatic dish. Rub the skin with sea salt and different vinegars for added crispiness and zest. Stock made from the carcase of an organic bird will be incomparably richer in flavour and colour and will set to a firmer jelly.

Game

Some game is farmed organically, including rabbit and venison. In a few parts of the world, other types of game, such as elk and wild boar are seasonally available, either from rural farmers' markets, or specialist suppliers. Animals and birds that are truly wild cannot be classified as organic, as their habitat and diet is not controlled or able to be inspected by an organic certifier. Wild game from areas with low agrochemically managed farmlands is unlikely to be contaminated with chemical pollutants.

Venison The term venison is used not only for meat from deer but also from elk, moose, reindeer, caribou and antelope. Deer are now farmed organically, but the demand for most farmed game animals is still too slow to stimulate a market.

Venison is a dark, close-textured meat with very little fat; what there is should be firm and white. If it is in good condition and a prime cut, such as

Above: Organic turkeys are free to exercise and are not fed growth hormones.

haunch, loin, fillet or best end, it will be juicy and tender and is best served rare. Other cuts, such as shoulder, neck and shin, are often marinated and benefit from long and gentle cooking to bring out the flavour of the meat.

Rabbit Fresh rabbit is a delicate well-flavoured meat, pale and mild in colour. It is high in protein, low in cholesterol and particularly low in fat. Organically farmed rabbit may be bought all the year round. It can be grilled (broiled), fried, roasted or stewed. Baste it well so that the meat does not dry out.

Wild Boar The meat of wild boar has a strong taste. It is dark in colour and, as there is little fat, it can be dry and tough, although the flavour is excellent. For this reason wild boar is usually marinated. It should be cooked in the same way as pork.

Game Birds Fresh game birds are only available during the hunting season, which varies from bird to bird and from country to country. In some countries frozen game is stocked all through the year. Simple

cooking methods are often the best for game birds: plain roasting for tender birds and simple casserole cooking for tougher birds. Organic butchers and direct suppliers will be able to provide useful cooking advice.

Pheasants are the most plentiful game birds and are often sold in a brace: a pair of birds that includes a male and a female. The hen is smaller and more tender than the cock. Organic partridge, grouse and quail are also available. Scottish grouse has a wonderful, rich flavour from feeding on the highland heather of Scotland, where it is native.

There are two types of partridge, the French or red-legged partridge, and the English, or grey-legged partridge. The red-legged bird is bigger but the flavour of the grey bird is often preferred.

Below: Wild boar has a strong taste and little fat.

FISH and SHELLFISH

Organic fish is a delicious source of protein and can be prepared and cooked very easily. Fresh fish is versatile and great for your health. Omega-3 essential fatty acids found naturally in oily fish help to lower cholesterol levels, protecting the heart and circulation system. Eating fish also reduces the risk of developing high blood pressure during pregnancy, and can help to prevent premature births. However, environmentally aware cooks need to shop with care.

Many fish are either caught using deeply environmentally insensitive methods or raised in unsustainable farms. Organic cooks should buy organically farmed fish or wild fish from sustainable farms and fisheries. If you have doubts about the source or sustainability of fish

Below: Organic fish is farmed using environmentally sensitive methods.

that you want to buy, write to or e-mail the head office of the retailer or processor to find out more. Every time an organization receives a letter of interest from a consumer, it is more likely to improve the sustainability of its practices. For information on the Internet, visit the web sites of organic certification bodies. You can ask good fishmongers or restaurateurs about the seafood they prepare, or contact a specialist organization such as the Marine Stewardship Council.

Farmed Fish

Organic fish farms are clean and humane. Chemicals are not permitted to be used routinely, although they may occasionally be administered if infection occurs. Many intensive fish farms need to douse their fish regularly in chemicals simply

Above: Pale, organically farmed salmon

because they are so intensive. The more fish are crammed into a body of water, the easier diseases such as furunculosis and parasites like fish lice can spread. Organic fish farmers keep numbers lower and the result is a radical reduction in disease and pestilence. There are some non-organic fish farms that do maintain healthier numbers, but buying organically farmed fish is the best way of being sure that the fish have been managed well.

Despite the many advantages, organic fish farming poses great challenges to pioneering organic aquaculture experts. To be certified as organic, fish must be fed fishmeal that is half a by-product of fish for human consumption, and half from sustainable sources. The trouble is, most fish by-products are from white fish such as cod. Farmed fish including salmon do not easily digest this sort of fishmeal, so there can be a lot of wasted food which then pollutes surrounding waters. Also, fishmeal from white fish has relatively low levels of fatty acids, so organically farmed fish can have relatively low levels of Omega-3 oils unless they are very carefully managed by an expert organic fish farmer. On the plus side, organically farmed fish are not permitted to be fed any genetically modified foods, so buying organic fish is the only way you can be certain that your farmed fish dinner is GM free.

Although good-quality non-organic salmon usually has relatively low levels of chemical residues, organically farmed salmon has even less. Organically

Right: Seawater fish farms produce excellent sea trout.

farmed fish are generally top class in terms of taste and texture, whereas intensively farmed fish are often bland and fatty. Organically farmed fish also have paler flesh. The stronger colour of non-organic farmed salmon is due to a diet based on fishmeal with added carotenoids. Although these are the same as the beneficial compounds found in carrots, organic cooks will prefer the more natural paler colour of organically farmed salmon.

Salmon, trout and carp taste wonderful grilled (broiled), steamed or fried in olive oil, especially when they are served with a generous squeeze of fresh lemon juice. Smoked in the traditional way, organically farmed fish have incomparable flavour, so different from the bland non-organic product, which is prepared using artificial wood smoke flavouring.

Below: MSC-certified halibut harvested by methods that protect the seabed.

Seawater Fish Farms

Organic seawater fish farms are beginning to rear many more breeds of fish. These include organic sea trout, bass, cod, halibut and bream. Humane and causing the minimum impact on the marine environment, organic sea fish farming is still in its infancy. As wild fish stocks come under increasing threat, this area of organic farming is set to grow.

There are currently only a few experimental organic prawn and shrimp farms, but this sector is certain to increase exponentially. Non-organic farmed prawns and shrimp farms tend to be the antithesis of the organic ideal, and have devastated large areas of the tropical world from the Indian Ocean to the mangroves of Honduras. Abusing the rights of local farmers who rear the crop, the prawn and shrimp industry often replaces rural diverse communities with a single polluting monoculture. To avoid adding to this type of situation, do not buy farmed prawns or shrimps unless they are certified as organic.

Such shellfish as cockles, mussels, scallops and oysters are sometimes farmed in enclosures around coastal seawaters. They feed on naturally occurring plankton and are a healthy source of food whose production has a low impact on the environment. Mussels and oysters are also a good source of betaine, a

substance that helps to protect against heart attacks. These shellfish are easy to prepare and make nutritious, high protein meals. Oysters should simply be prised open with a knife and eaten whole, with a squirt of lemon. Clean mussels by scrubbing them in fresh water and pulling off any fibrous "beards" that sprout between the two halves of the shell. Discard any mussels which are open or fail to snap shut when tapped with a knife.

Left: Organic mussels and other shellfish are increasingly farmed in enclosures around coastal seawaters.

There is no organic standard for wild fish. However, the MSC – Marine Stewardship Council – is a certifying body that is beginning to address the issue. It is a leading voice in the sustainable fishing debate, and offers practical guidance to consumers, fishermen and governments alike.

When certifying a fishery, the MSC looks at three areas of activity. First, the state of the fish stocks in the locality is assessed to determine whether fishing is being carried out sustainably. The fishery's effect on the marine ecosystem is also looked at. One major problem of modern fishing methods is catching fish other than the target species – the "by-catch". The MSC standard is only awarded if levels of by-catch for the fishery are acceptable. Finally, management systems are examined to satisfy the MSC that good practice is being maintained.

Fishermen often work under an umbrella organization, which may be a government body, that regulates the area of the sea they harvest. If good management is in place, their practices can be co-ordinated to ensure sustainable fishing.

Buying MSC-certified Fish

A secondary certification scheme traces all fish certified to the MSC standard from the fishery to the retailer, so consumers can buy wild fish with confidence if it carries the MSC logo. You will find the logo on fresh and frozen fish, convenience products and on menus where restaurants support the scheme.

MSC-certified fish is sold through independent fishmongers, farmers' markets, supermarkets and delicatessens in the UK and Europe, USA and Australia. Fish caught at MSC-certified fisheries are also sold in Canada, New Zealand and South East Asian countries. However, not all these countries use the logo.

Wild Fish

The last major wild food resource, the sea, is under intense threat from over-fishing. Worldwide, sea fish are now so over-exploited that many once abundant stocks are now under threat of extinction. Catching wild fish has become a serious technological pursuit. Wild sea fish are hunted with the aid of radar, planes and submarines and caught with lines or trawler nets, trapping the targeted catch and also other fish, mammals and birds. These wholesale raids do not discriminate between adults and young fish.

Wild fish are increasingly subjected to chemical, biological and hormonal attack from such polluted fresh waters as rivers and lakes. Some intensive fish farms release their waste water, with its cargo of chemicals and germs, into nearby rivers and seas. Fish from these farms often escape and interbreed with wild stocks to produce hybrid mutations. Pesticides and fertilizers from agrochemical crops also flow into rivers and lakes through groundwater. The fertilizers promote algae growth, ruining the delicate balance of water ecosystems, while pesticides simply poison the inhabitants.

Wild salmon spend almost all of their lives in the sea, only returning to fresh water when it is time to spawn. They have incredible homing instincts.

Above: Wild salmon live in the sea, returning to fresh water only when it is time to spawn.

A salmon that has swum hundreds of kilometres away from its birthplace will return to the very creek where its life began. If the water it has to pass through has been contaminated by fish farm, agrochemical farm or factory pollution, this ancient cycle is irrevocably disturbed.

Types of Wild Sea Fish

Wild sea fish fall into two groups: those that live at the bottom of the sea, and those that live in the middle waters or near the surface. Surface fish include common varieties such as sardines, mackerel, anchovies, pilchards, Atlantic herring and swordfish. Fishermen utilize many methods to catch these fish, including traps, lines and drag nets. In Japan, fishermen sometimes lure squid using mechanical jiggers with bright lights. The squid attach themselves to the machinery, so they can be hauled on to the boats easily. Knowledgeable fishermen easily target surface species, ensuring a good percentage of the catch is the target fish. Despite this, many of these species are now fully or over fished.

Fish species from the middle waters include tuna, salmon and herring. These fish are almost always caught with nets.

Tuna are a similar size to dolphins and often associate with them. In the past, this frequently meant that when tuna were caught, so were dolphins. The public outcry that ensued when this became common knowledge has diminished this practice. All tuna sold in the USA and Canada now has to be dolphin friendly, and most other industrialized nations offer dolphin-friendly tuna.

Catching tuna without catching dolphins is very tricky however. One technique that has replaced dolphin-associated tuna fishing is to use floating aggregate devices, or FADs. These float in the sea and attract the tuna because of the cover they provide. Fishermen then net all of the fish below the FAD, including juvenile tuna and other by-catch species. Although dolphin-friendly tuna does save dolphins, it is often at the expense of other species with a less popular public image.

Probably the best way to catch tuna in terms of the ecosystem is with so-called "long lines". These fishing lines with multiple hooks are dragged behind boats and target tuna extremely efficiently. Some successful long-line tuna fisheries use this method, including one in the Maldives that supplies retailers and restaurants around the world.

Below: Wild cockles can be picked by hand.

Fish that live on the bottom of the sea are generally trawled with big nets. Cod, carp, hake, haddock, hoki and Alaskan pollock all live near the seabed, as do flat fish including plaice, halibut and sole. Cephalopods such as squid and octopus are often also trapped in the nets, but offer a valuable source of under-exploited seafood. Trawling the seabed can be extremely destructive, disturbing ancient ecosystems. The Marine Stewardship Council has approved one fishery that trawls responsibly, and more fisheries that use other sustainable harvesting methods for species at the bottom of the sea. Fisheries awarded MSC certification are sustainable, so you can be sure that buying these products will not contribute to bad fishing practices.

Shellfish

Lobsters and crabs also live at the bottom of the sea but they are only harvested in coastal waters. They are usually collected in pots, either using bait or trapdoors. Scallops and oysters, which also live in coastal waters, are traditionally trawled. Today, they are often harvested by divers. This method protects the delicate ecosystems found at the bottom of the sea, while providing top quality seafood for the caring cook. Other shellfish such as wild cockles and mussels are more easily harvested. They can be picked by hand from the bottom of shallower waters. However, most commercially available shellfish are currently farmed.

Intensively farmed prawns and shrimps are bad news for organic consumers. Try to buy wild shellfish. Those from Iceland are particularly acceptable as an alternative to organically farmed prawns and shrimps. Iceland is heavily reliant on its fishing industry, so it has become a benchmark country for sustainable fishing techniques. Most prawns from Iceland are caught by trawling with nets with bigger holes than other fishing nations. The holes allow young prawns to escape, so they can grow and breed.

MOULES MARINIÈRE

1 Chop 1 onion and 2 shallots. Put in a large pan with 25g/1oz/2 tbsp butter and cook over low heat until softened and translucent.

2 Add 300ml/½ pint/1¼ cups white wine, a bay leaf and a sprig of fresh thyme. Bring to the boil. Add 2kg/4½lb cleaned mussels, cover the pan tightly and steam over a high heat for 2 minutes. Shake the pan vigorously and steam for 2 minutes more. Shake again and steam until all the mussels have opened. Discard any closed shells.

3 Stir in 30ml/2 tbsp chopped fresh parsley and serve at once.

DAIRY FOODS and EGGS

Opting for organic products means obtaining the maximum nutrition from whatever dairy foods you consume, without supporting the negative aspects associated with intensive farming methods. Dairy foods are excellent sources of protein and calcium.

On an organic dairy farm, cows have regular access to open fields. Their diet is made up almost exclusively of organic grasses and grains and they are never routinely treated with the hormones that are used on non-organic farms in some countries to boost milk production. Nor are they dosed with antibiotics except as a last resort. If you prefer not to eat any dairy foods, there are some excellent organic alternatives.

Milk

Organic milk is the only kind of milk that is guaranteed to be free of genetically modified ingredients, as many non-organic cows eat GM feed. It is available with varying amounts of cream, from skimmed to full fat. Full fat (whole) milk generally only contains about 2 percent fat, so all milk is a low fat food. Most milk is pasteurized, homogenized or sterilized, but it can also be found raw. Pasteurization is a heating process that helps to control bacteria levels in the milk. Homogenization distributes

Right: Goat's, cow's, sheep's and soya milk

the fat content throughout the milk, so there is no need to shake it to mix in the cream. Sterilization extends the shelf life of sealed cartons of milk, so that they do not need to be refrigerated. All these processes are permitted under organic certification laws because they are mechanical processes that do not involve the use of chemicals.

Cow's milk is not the only organic option. Goat's milk has a distinctive, musky flavour, which many people love. It is much easier to digest than cow's milk, so individuals who cannot tolerate cow's milk often find they can drink goat's milk without suffering adverse reactions. Organic sheep's milk is sometimes on sale at the larger farmer's markets or in delicatessens. It doesn't taste as pungent as goat's milk, but contains more of the lactose that can cause dairy intolerance.

Yogurts, Creams and Dairy Desserts

Live yogurt is a natural probiotic. This means it boosts the amount of beneficial bacteria in the intestines of those who eat it. This, in turn, aids the absorption of nutrients, such as calcium, as well as offering some protection from various disorders, including tooth decay and

heart disease. An even better way of improving the levels of good bacteria in your gut is to eat prebiotic foods such as onions, leeks, wheat, oats, bananas and Jerusalem artichokes.

Many of the world's largest non-organic dairy corporations now also offer organic yogurts, creams and dairy desserts. While this ensures improved availability of organic dairy products, the quality is variable. Organic dairy products all have the benefits of humane and environmentally sustainable production, but mass-produced yogurts and dairy desserts are often watery, high in sugar and low in flavour. Whether they are runny or thick, organic creams should always be mouthwateringly rich. The organic connoisseur will choose organic yogurts, desserts and creams from smaller enterprises or companies who are primarily organic.

Butter

Organic butter has a much richer taste than non-organic alternatives. Both types, however, are equally high in saturated fats, which can raise cholesterol levels in the body and contribute to heart disease. Consider organic butter a luxurious, delicious and slightly decadent treat, great for the occasional indulgence, as when making the perfect fried egg, but something to be limited. That said, organic butter is far better for your health than many non-organic margarines and spreads. These will often contain hydrogenated or trans fats, which may be far more damaging to the heart than butter.

Right: Organic butter

Cheeses

Organic cheeses are made from organic milk, so they offer all the environmental, humanitarian and healthy eating benefits of other organic dairy products. They come in scores of different varieties, from hard types such as Cheddar, Cheshire, Double Gloucester and Lancashire, through blues like Stilton and Gorgonzola, to soft and creamy Camembert and cottage cheese. Lots of artisan cheesemakers now use organic ingredients. Buying organic cheese is a must if you want to avoid eating genetically modified rennet.

Soya Milk and Other Substitutes

Soya beans have been transformed into nutritious "milks" and dairy alternative foods for thousands of years. There are dozens of versions on the market, including the fresh product, which looks like cow's milk but is slightly thicker and has a nutty taste. More readily available is long-life soya milk, which comes in cartons and does not need to be refrigerated until it is opened. Sweetened versions can also be found, and it is possible to buy soya milk that has been fortified with extra vitamins as well as calcium.

Soya milk is low in calories and contains no cholesterol. Easy to digest, it is a valuable food, particularly for those who cannot tolerate cow's milk. Children who suffer from asthma and eczema often get relief when they switch from cow's milk to a non-dairy alternative such as soya milk.

Soya cream is much thicker and richer than soya milk because it is made with a higher proportion of beans.

Soya beans are not the only ingredient that can be made into nutritious liquid. Other beans can be used in a similar way, as can some nuts and grains. Rice milk is thin and has a delicate taste. Tiger nut milk has a similar consistency and a sweet taste. Oat milk is pleasantly mild, while pale yellow pea milk is quite creamy. Non-dairy milks can be bought from health food shops or made at home. Try them on muesli or other organic cereals or in creamy soups. When using in tea, put non-dairy milk in first and stir the tea thoroughly to prevent curdling. The high acidity in coffee means that curdling is almost inevitable, so try to avoid using non-dairy milks here.

Above: Organic Stilton and Brie are widely available.

Eggs

Organic free-range eggs come from hens that have ample access to land free from chemical fertilizers and pesticides. The birds are not routinely debeaked to stop them retaliating when hemmed in by other hens, nor are they given growth promoters. Antibiotics are administered only when unavoidable. It is important to look for labels on eggs that attest to organic certification. Although the term "free range" suggests that hens spend their days out of doors, non-organic free-range birds often have limited access to the open air. Organic eggs are the only eggs that can be guaranteed to be free from yolk colourants.

Look out for other types of eggs at farmers' markets. Duck eggs are a pretty shade of blue, goose eggs are big enough for two and quail's eggs are small and speckled. All can be boiled, fried, scrambled or used in cakes, in the same way as hen's eggs. When soft-boiled, organic eggs are far less likely to contain the salmonella that is often found in eggs from intensive chicken barns. Soft-boiled or lightly poached eggs have the advantage of containing fewer Cholesterol Oxidation Products (COPS), which means they can be beneficial to blood cholesterol levels.

Below: When farmed organically, quail and duck eggs are guaranteed free from yolk colourants.

THE ORGANIC STORE CUPBOARD

A well stocked store cupboard is a valuable asset for any cook, but it is absolutely essential for the organic cook, who may not be able to obtain every ingredient at the last minute by simply popping down to the local store.

It is worth spending a bit of time sourcing organic food. There is already a lot of it out there, and with more and more products becoming available all the time, switching to organic ingredients is relatively easy. You don't have to do it all at once; simply replace non-organic oils, vinegars, jams, nuts, seasonings and other items in your store cupboard with organic alternatives when they run out. A good organic stockist with a rapid turnover is a good place to start, and the Internet can be handy, too.

Sugars and Honeys

Organic sugars are beneficial because they do not cause the pollution to developing countries that agrochemically grown versions often do. Refined and unrefined organic versions of all standard sugars except refined white are readily available, from demerara (raw) to soft brown. Unrefined organic sugars have far fewer vitamins and nutrients stripped out of them during processing than

Below: Molasses is a great source of iron.

Above: Rapadura is an excellent organic alternative to refined sugar.

refined sugars, and for this reason they have a slightly better flavour, too. That said, organic sugar still has a high empty calorie value, so it should always be used sparingly for a healthy balanced diet.

Rapadura This exciting alternative to refined sugar is only available in organic form. Similar in colour and texture to soft brown sugar, it has a much more interesting flavour and nutrient profile because it is made by simply sun-drying organic sugar cane juice, so all the beneficial vitamins and minerals of this natural product are retained. Rapadura is suitable for any style of cooking that calls for sugar, including jam-making and meringues. It is also known as jaggery, the Hindi name for this product.

Molasses Another excellent natural sweetener derived from sugar cane is molasses. Organic molasses has all the minerals in sugar cane in concentrated form, and is a great source of iron. The most nutritionally valuable type is thick and very dark blackstrap molasses. The powerful taste of molasses makes it a good choice for treacly biscuits, cakes, puddings and sauces.

Honey The most popular alternative to refined sugar is honey. Organic honey must come from unpolluted areas if it is to retain its purity. Most non-organic honey comes from bees fed on liquid sugar rather than collecting pollen. It is inferior to the organic version, both in its blandness and its lack of nutrition.

There are some wonderful organic honeys, each reflecting the flavours of the flowering plants visited by the bees. From Australian manuka honey to Zimbabwean forest honey, the choices range from powerful dark solid honeys to delicate golden liquid honeys. It is worth tasting a selection to discover your personal favourite, and familiarizing yourself with each variety so you can select the ideal match when cooking. Try using honey instead of syrup or sugar in cakes, or giving a hint of sweetness to salad dressings and hot sauces.

Honey has long been highly valued for its medicinal and healing properties. Mixed with lemon juice and hot water, it has antiseptic properties and can relieve sore throats. It is also thought to be helpful in treating diarrhoea and asthma.

Left: Organic farmers' markets are a good place to seek out unusual and homemade organic jams, marmalades, honeys, pickles and preserves.

Above: *Fruit syrups are natural sweeteners, which can be used in place of sugar.*

Other Natural Sweeteners

There are lots of other sweetening options for the organic cook to explore including organic maple syrup, maple sugar and a wide range of fruit products.
Maple Syrup and Sugar Made by tapping the sap of the maple tree, organic maple syrup and sugar are not over-processed, so retain their richness. Drizzled over hot pancakes, maple, with its buttery tones, is the ultimate syrup. A small amount, added to a savoury batter, tantalizes the palate. Maple syrup is sweeter than sugar so less is required in cooking.
Fruit Syrups and Pastes Concentrated organic fruit syrups also make great sweeteners, whether you choose the liquid form or the solid paste. They contain none of

Above: *A selection of organic honeys*

the pesticides found in agrochemical versions and no added sugar or preservatives. They are just as popular with children as with adults. Concentrates are made from many types of organic fruit, including apples, pears, grapes, dates, peaches, blackcurrants and oranges. Apple and date versions add most sweetness, so can be used more sparingly than some other types. Their flavours are also not particularly dominant, so they will not overwhelm other ingredients. Pastes can also be used in cooking, but will need to be dissolved in water first. On their own, fruit pastes taste delicious when spread on bread. Most organic outlets sell concentrated fruit syrups and pastes. They can be stored in a refrigerator for 2–3 months.

Puréed dried fruits such as prunes, figs, dates and apricots can also be used to sweeten pies, crumbles and cakes. To make spiced apricot purée, place some apricots in a pan with enough water to cover, add a cinnamon stick, two cloves and a little freshly grated nutmeg, and simmer for 20 minutes until the apricots are plump. Leave to cool then purée in a food processor until smooth. Add more water if the mixture seems a little thick.

Above: *Organic chocolate comes in dark, white and milk varieties.*

Cocoa and Chocolate

Agrochemical cocoa is the most heavily sprayed food crop, and is often unfairly traded, too. By buying organic cocoa and chocolate products you ensure that you are not supporting agrochemical pollution in developing countries.

Organic chocolate products are usually higher in cocoa and lower in sugar than the non-organic equivalent, and are free from hydrogenated fats, emulsifiers and other chemical additives. Organic cocoa is naturally high in tannins and antioxidant flavonoids, plus B vitamins and iron. This means that eating organic chocolate in moderation can do you good, as it is thought to offer some protection against heart attacks.

The darker the chocolate, the higher the percentage of cocoa solids and the more intense the taste. Chocolate with 70 per cent cocoa solids has a proportionally higher nutritional content.

Organic chocolate comes in a wide array of products, from specialist hand-made pralines to slabs of dark (bittersweet), milk and white and flavoured chocolates. They all keep well and can be stored in the refrigerator, so there is no need to eat all the chocolate at once.

Nuts and Seeds

Organic nuts and seeds are little powerhouses that would grow into new plants or mighty trees if sown and allowed to germinate. This makes them an incredibly rich source of nutrients. High in plant oils and protein, they also yield B complex vitamins, potassium, magnesium, calcium, phosphorus and iron. The fat they contain is largely monounsaturated or polyunsaturated (only coconuts and brazil nuts contain saturated fat) and they are the richest vegetable source of vitamin E, which has been credited with reducing the risk of heart disease, strokes and certain cancers.

Many people equate a healthy diet with a low fat diet, but this is not true. It is important that we eat a balanced diet, including proteins, carbohydrates and fats. While saturated and hydrogenated fats are undesirable, unrefined polyunsaturated fats are essential. They provide energy and help to prevent heart disease, eczema, ulcers and arthritis when eaten as part of a healthy diet and combined with a balanced lifestyle. The best way of obtaining polyunsaturated fats is to eat nuts and seeds, since these also provide the antioxidants necessary to optimise the value of these fats.

Seeds are very good for you for many other reasons, too. Sunflower seeds are rich in many minerals, including zinc, which aids skin regeneration and helps to heal cuts and minor abrasions. The

Walnuts (above) and hazelnuts (below) are a good source of protein.

seeds also contain B vitamins and will ease fatigue, irritability and depression. Flax (linseed) seeds are gentle healers for the intestinal tract. Sesame seeds are a good source of protein, zinc and iron, so are good for sexual health. Pumpkin seeds have similar nutrients, plus calcium and B vitamins.

Cooking With Organic Nuts And Seeds

Health reasons aside, organic nuts and seeds taste great. You can add chopped nuts and seeds to salads, savoury roasts, breads and cakes. Roasting nuts and seeds in a dry, non-stick frying pan for

MAKING NUT BUTTER

Nut butters don't have to contain just one type of nut. Make your own wholesome nut butter using a combination of organic peanuts, hazelnuts and cashew nuts.

1 Place 75g/3oz/½ cup shelled nuts in a food processor or blender and process until finely ground.

2 Pour 15–30ml/1–2 tbsp sunflower oil into the processor or blender and process to a coarse paste. Spread on toast or stir into stir-fries to produce a rich, creamy sauce. Store in an airtight container.

Above: *Peanuts*

Right: *Organic chestnuts are sweet and starchy.*

NUT NOTES

The perfect snack food, nuts provide plenty of nutrients, too.

• Brazil nuts are a good source of protein, with lots of vitamin B₁ and magnesium to aid concentration and support the nervous system.

• Walnuts contain as much protein as eggs, plus potassium, zinc and iron.

• Pecan nuts, walnuts and hemp seeds are a source of linoleic acid, which has anti-inflammatory properties. Smokers who have kicked the habit find it soothes lungs irritated by the free radicals in cigarette smoke. These nuts and seeds are also a first line of defence against other forms of cancer, because of their high vitamin E content, plus the fact that they are the only known sources of an antioxidant group called avenanthramides. People who eat walnuts or pecans five times a week have been discovered to lower their risk of developing coronary heart disease by 35 per cent.

• Pine nuts are the richest source of protein of any nut, with a deliciously buttery flavour that makes them great in salads.

• Peanuts are a good source of both iron and protein.

• Hazelnuts have a sweet flavour but are relatively low in calories.

• Chestnuts are sweet and starchy, and help to bind other ingredients, in nut roasts or stuffings, for instance.

Below: Black and white sesame seeds

a few minutes greatly improves the flavour. Watch them carefully and toss frequently so that they don't scorch.

Store-bought non-organic nut butters, including peanut butter, often contain unwanted hydrogenated oil and can be loaded with sugar, so buy organic nut or seed butters. Alternatively, make your own by processing your favourite nuts and seeds through a masticating juicer or in a food processor or blender.

Tahini, made by grinding sesame seeds, is especially good. Stir tahini or nut butter into a stir-fry for an instant sauce. When used in this way, nut and seed butters become favourite seasonings. When spread on toast, they make nutritious and very tasty toppings.

Oils

Cold pressed organic oils retain almost all the health and taste benefits of the raw nuts and seeds from which they are made. This is not the case with most agrochemical oils, which are extracted at high temperatures. In the process the natural antioxidants, minerals and other vitamins in the oil are destroyed. Non-organic oil is then further processed with solvents to lessen the colour and tone down the taste of the final product. Cold-pressed organic oils are prized for these very characteristics.

Olive oil is a firm favourite. In terms of colour and taste, it is a wonderful addition to any meal. It is a versatile food that can be eaten alone on bread instead of butter, added to salads or used for cooking, and is the perfect partner for organic food. It is the most digestible oil, and is universally acknowledged as being highly effective in preventing heart disease and treating liver disorders. Many nut oils make delicious salad dressings when whisked with lemon juice or vinegar. Organic sunflower and safflower oils are rich in polyunsaturates that are great for heart health. Use them in dishes that require a lighter taste than olive oil, such as in oriental cooking and cake baking.

Above: Pumpkin seeds make a perfect organic snack food.

Storing Nuts, Seeds and Oils

Buy nuts in the shell, if possible, and eat them as soon as possible after shelling. If you must store them, put them in airtight bags and keep them in a cool place or the refrigerator. Store seeds in the same way. Buy cold pressed organic oils in small quantities, so that they can be used quickly, and store in a cool place. Never allow them to be exposed to heat during storage. Do not store nuts, seeds or oils for more than a few months, or the oil they contain may become rancid.

Above: Cold-pressed organic sunflower and safflower oils

SEASONINGS

If you are new to organic cooking, you may find you need to rethink your approach to seasonings of all kinds. Organic ingredients taste so good that to mask their flavours would be a sin. Use spices, condiments and strong flavourings such as vinegar with care, choosing always the organic option.

Spices

Over sixty different kinds of spices are regularly used in cooking around the world. About twenty of these are easily available organically grown. Try to find organic spices where you can, because non-organic ones have often been heavily sprayed with pesticides. Most of these plants are grown in developing countries where non-organic farming practices can undermine farmers' health and the environment. Until recently dried spices with organic certification were quite difficult to track down. Now they are much more readily available, in good organic stores, direct from the packers or through mail order companies.

Spices are almost always used dried when their flavours are condensed. However, fresh versions of chillies and ginger are also popular. Organic dried chillies are a useful store-cupboard ingredient. They come whole, powdered or in flakes and tend to be hotter than fresh chillies. Especially valuable chillies include fruity, mild anchos, chipotles and hot habaneros.

Below: Fresh organic root ginger has an intense fiery flavour.

Above: Organic dried chillies are free from harmful pesticide residues.

Fry dried spices before adding them to a dish. Heat a pan with or without oil and fry or toast the spices for about 1 minute, until they release their aroma. Shake the pan often to prevent them from sticking. Most spices should be toasted whole, then crushed with a pestle in a mortar or whizzed in a coffee blender. However such spices as nutmeg and cinnamon are too large or bulky to be heated whole. Crush cinnamon bark or grate whole nutmeg just before toasting it. These spices retain more flavour when they are stored whole.

Fresh organic root ginger is smaller and has a more intense flavour than the swollen and sometimes watery non-organic spice. Ginger and galangal add a hot yet refreshing flavour to sweet and savoury dishes, including marinades, stir-fries, fresh vegetables, poached fruit and cakes and bakes.

The five spices most often used in Indian cooking are coriander, cumin, turmeric, pepper and chilli. Many other spices are used alongside this quintet, including star anise and fenugreek. Try adding nutmeg to savoury dishes such as pumpkin soup and baked fish as well as more traditional sweet dishes such as Christmas pudding or rice pudding. The powerful essential oils in this spice have slightly euphoric properties, so they lift the spirits. No wonder nutmeg is a popular spice in mulled wine and other festive Christmas treats. Add caraway seeds to sauerkraut or bean stews, as they help to ease flatulence. Coriander seeds can help to cool an otherwise hot and spicy dish, as well as adding their distinctive flavour. Chilli powder acts like cornflour (cornstarch), thickening stews and curries, and pepper adds accent to almost everything, including strawberries.

Salt

The main flavouring used in cooking throughout the world is salt. At one time this was guaranteed to be a natural product extracted from seawater. Table salt is now almost exclusively over-refined, with magnesium carbonate

---

PREPARING FRESH GINGER

1 You don't need to peel fresh organic root ginger. Using a small, sharp paring knife, simply chop to the size specified in the recipe.

2 Alternatively, grate ginger finely. Special bamboo graters can be found in many Asian stores, but an ordinary box grater will do the job equally well. Freshly grated ginger can be squeezed with the fingers to release the juice, if required.

added to ensure it flows freely. Sea salt, whether organically certified or not, has a much broader spectrum of taste because it contains a variety of different minerals and salts alongside the sodium chloride that is its main component. Keep your salt usage low, as using too much of this mineral compound can lead to high blood pressure. One benefit of using good-quality salt is that it has a stronger flavour, so you do not need to use as much salt. Organically certified salts are particularly delicious and it is most reassuring to know that such salts are routinely inspected by the certifier whose logo they bear.

Left: Sea salt contains a variety of minerals and salts.

Right: Wholegrain organic mustard.

Right: Organic light and dark shoyu (soy sauce) adds flavour.

Soy Sauces

Many organic cooks use organic soy sauces such as tamari and shoyu to add saltiness and depth to their meals. These products will enhance the flavour of most savoury dishes, but should be added in moderation, at the end of the cooking process. High temperatures destroy the delicate proteins and enzymes that are so beneficial in these products.

Vinegars

Organic vinegars are made by fermenting ingredients such as organic apples and grapes. Over time, these fine ingredients will develop into zesty condiments to be drizzled over fish or added to salad dressings, pickles and marinades. There

are plenty of organic varieties, including balsamic and Japanese mirin rice vinegar.

Some non-organic vinegars are good-quality products, with fine flavours and good fragrances. However, many non-organic vinegars are horrible. The vinegar in most of England's famous fish and chip shops bears little resemblance to good, old-fashioned malt vinegar.

At the opposite end of the spectrum is organic cider vinegar. This raw, unfiltered, non-distilled, undiluted product is aged in wooden barrels and contains no preservatives, and has superb health benefits. It is antibacterial, antiseptic, anti-inflammatory and detoxifying. It also helps to keep blood thin, which is useful for people who eat meat and dairy products.

Other Condiments

Many condiments contain vinegar as a major ingredient, including mustard, prepared salad dressings, mayonnaise, chutneys, pickles and olives. The benefits of buying organic versions of these products are obvious, since you can be sure that a good vinegar has been used as a base. Other ingredients will be organic, too, so whatever you buy is likely to be flavoursome and of good quality. The eggs in organic mayonnaise will have come from free-range organic chickens. Vegan organic mayonnaise is also readily available, made from soy or pea protein. The taste of some organic full grain mustards puts regular non-organic mustards to shame. While many non-organic commercial salad dressings threaten to drown your healthy leaves in refined, sugary oils, organic salad dressings have been known to outshine a home-made mixture. Although the best chutneys and pickles are made in your kitchen, there are plenty of excellent ones available in supermarkets, farmers' markets and good organic stores.

Above: Cider vinegar is antibacterial.

DRINKS

Over the past decade or so, the demand for organic drinks has grown enormously. From a niche market, the beverage industry has burgeoned, producing drinks that are often so delicious that even those who are not yet fully committed to the organic ideal seek them out. From table water to gin, an organic certification mark on the bottle is a sign of fine quality and sustainable ingredients.

Below, left to right: Organic biodynamic white and red wines and elderflower wine

Wine

Organic wine is an explosion of flavours. Very often produced by small artisan vineyards, the organic grapes used in organic wines are much more diverse than those found in the majority of standard non-organic wines. Hangovers are usually caused by sulphites, which can also provoke asthma and migraines. Levels of sulphur are much lower in organic wines, so you really can feel the difference the next day. Organic vineyards recycle their waste grape skins by

composting them, and they often plant flowering plants among the vines to attract pollinating insects and predators.

Prizewinning organic and biodynamic red and white wines are produced all over the world, including in France, Italy, Australia and California. Red wine is full of health-promoting antioxidants, so it is good for preventing heart disease as well as relieving stress if drunk in moderation.

To find a good supplier of organic wine, contact an independent wine dealer. The Internet is an invaluable tool for finding such retailers; simply make a search for organic wine dealers and look for one in your area. Alternatively, buy the wines direct from the vineyard.

Fruit wines can also be delicious. Organic stores sell several varieties, but the best way to investigate the many delights of elderberry, elderflower and blackcurrant wine is to make your own. Home wine-making kits can be used with organic ingredients to produce excellent results.

Store organic wine on its side in a cool, dark place to keep the cork moist. Try adding your favourite wines to sauces and fruit salads, or organic sherry and port to trifles and cakes.

Spirits

Wines are not the only prizewinning organic drinks. Some incredible spirits are available, including industry award winners such as Del Meguey mezcal. This organic mezcal is produced by traditional artisans in Mexico who have had the craft passed down to them through countless generations. Del Meguey produce five kinds of organic mezcal, with their top-of-the-range product achieving international status as one of the finest spirits in the world.

Organic gin and vodka have also reached a fine quality now, with Juniper Green gin and UK5 vodka made in London, England. Distilled from organic raw ingredients, you will find that these spirits have a clean, round taste, with lots of warm flavours in the gin. You can also buy organic Scotch whisky, plus more unusual spirits including Grappa and Calvados.

Beer and Cider

Organic beer and lager microbreweries have sprung up and begun to flourish all over the world, from North America to Belgium and Germany. The intensity that organic hops impart to the flavour of organic beers and lagers has encouraged the general trend towards high quality traditional brews. There are dark stouts and light lagers, bronze bitters and extra strong Belgian beers. There is even a German hemp beer, Cannabia, based on an ancient Roman recipe.

Organic ciders are made from organic apples, and often contain much less added sulphur dioxide than non-organic ciders. This makes them less likely to provoke hangovers in the morning. The largest range of organic cider is currently produced in England, but they are also brewed commercially in France.

Serve cider cold with a hot pork dinner or ham lunch. Alternatively, add a little to the pan when roasting lamb for additional flavour and acidity.

Water

The ultimate soft drink is water. Essential for human health, it is undeniably the most thirst-quenching drink of them all. Add a squeeze of lemon juice or a sprig of fresh mint, and it becomes even more enjoyable. Although bottled water cannot be certified as organic, the label can state that it was sourced from organically farmed land. This is important if you want to avoid pesticides that may have run off agrochemical farmland into the water table beneath.

Tap water quality varies hugely between regions, depending on the geology of the area and its filtration capabilities. At best, it is pure and full of beneficial minerals such as calcium. At worst, it can contain pesticides, hormones and heavy metals.

Water Filters The best way to ensure that the water you drink is as pure as possible is to invest in a good-quality water filter. There are many variations on three basic types. The most common is the carbon filter, which is good at cleaning most impurities, including fluoride. An even better version incorporates a built-in reverse osmosis system that guarantees absolute purity from all heavy metals and other pollutants. Distillers are

Left to right: Organic Juniper Green gin, made in London and German hemp beer, Cannabia

Above: Fresh organic lemonade

also available, but the water they produce must be supplemented carefully with minerals from foods or supplements. Choosing organic drinks is a good way of avoiding additives, but drinking pure water is even better.

Fizzy Drinks

If you want to enjoy fizzy drinks or sodas as part of an organic diet it is essential that the drinks you buy are also organic. Non-organic colas are universally bad for your health. Although it is usual for both organic and non-organic fizzy drinks to contain a very high proportion of sugar, the non-organic drinks are full of artificial chemical additives that are seriously undermining. The phosphoric acid in colas is directly related to loss of calcium in bone. This can lead to osteoporosis, a disease that is becoming more common throughout the industrialized world.

Non-organic diet drinks usually contain synthetic sweeteners such as aspartame and saccharine. These artificial additives are strictly banned in organic foods, with very good reason. Aspartame is a neurotoxin that affects the appetite control centres in the brain. As a result, serotonin levels in the brain drop, often leading to depression. Consumers of artificially sweetened drinks often have difficulty dieting.

ORGANIC RECIPES

All the recipes in this section show how mouthwatering

dishes can be prepared simply and easily with fresh

seasonal produce. There are ideas for every occasion, and

all recipes are as delicious as they are healthy. There are

suggestions for soups, starters and salads, hearty main

courses and tempting desserts as well as cakes and bakes.

If you love cooking and eating good food, you will

discover that organic produce offers an exciting choice.

With this fabulous selection of recipes, you will have all

the advice and inspiration you need to make

a delicious, healthy meal.

WINTER FARMHOUSE SOUP

Root vegetables form the base of this chunky, minestrone-style main meal soup.
Always choose organic vegetables and vary according to what you have to hand.

SERVES FOUR

30ml/2 tbsp olive oil
1 onion, roughly chopped
3 carrots, cut into large chunks
175–200g/6–7oz turnips, cut into
    large chunks
about 175g/6oz swede (rutabaga), cut into
    large chunks
400g/14oz can chopped Italian tomatoes
15ml/1 tbsp tomato purée (paste)
5ml/1 tsp dried mixed herbs
5ml/1 tsp dried oregano
50g/2oz dried (bell) peppers, washed and
    thinly sliced (optional)
1.5 litres/2½ pints/6¼ cups vegetable
    stock or water
50g/2oz/½ cup dried macaroni
400g/14oz can red kidney beans, rinsed
    and drained
30ml/2 tbsp chopped fresh flat leaf parsley
sea salt and ground black pepper
freshly grated Parmesan cheese or premium
    Italian-style vegetarian cheese, to serve

1 Heat the olive oil in a large pan, add the onion and cook over a low heat for about 5 minutes until softened. Add the carrot, turnip and swede chunks, canned chopped tomatoes, tomato purée, dried mixed herbs, dried oregano and dried peppers, if using. Stir in a little salt and plenty of pepper to taste.

2 Pour in the vegetable stock or water and bring to the boil. Stir well, cover the pan, then lower the heat and simmer for 30 minutes, stirring occasionally.

3 Add the pasta to the pan and bring quickly to the boil, stirring. Lower the heat and simmer, uncovered, for about 8 minutes until the pasta is only just tender, or according to the instructions on the packet. Stir frequently.

4 Stir in the kidney beans. Heat through for 2–3 minutes, then remove the pan from the heat and stir in the parsley. Taste the soup for seasoning. Serve hot in warmed soup bowls, with grated cheese handed separately.

MOROCCAN SPICED MUTTON SOUP

Classic north African spices – ginger, turmeric and cinnamon – are combined with chickpeas and mutton to make this hearty, warming main-course soup.

SERVES SIX

75g/3oz/½ cup chickpeas, soaked overnight
15g/½oz/1 tbsp butter or 15ml/1 tbsp
   olive oil
225g/8oz mutton, cut into cubes
1 onion, chopped
450g/1lb tomatoes, peeled and chopped
a few celery leaves, chopped
30ml/2 tbsp chopped fresh parsley
15ml/1 tbsp chopped fresh coriander
   (cilantro)
2.5ml/½ tsp ground ginger
2.5ml/½ tsp ground turmeric
5ml/1 tsp ground cinnamon
1.75 litres/3 pints/7½ cups water
75g/3oz/scant ½ cup green lentils
75g/3oz/¾ cup vermicelli or soup pasta
2 egg yolks
juice of ½–1 lemon, to taste
sea salt and ground black pepper
fresh coriander (cilantro), to garnish
lemon wedges, to serve

1 Drain the chickpeas and set aside. Heat the butter or oil in a large pan and fry the mutton and onion for 2–3 minutes, stirring, until the mutton is just browned.

2 Add the chopped tomatoes, celery leaves, herbs and spices and season well with ground black pepper. Cook for about 1 minute, then stir in the water and add the green lentils and the soaked, drained and rinsed chickpeas.

3 Slowly bring to the boil and skim the surface to remove the froth. Boil rapidly for 10 minutes, then reduce the heat and simmer very gently for 2 hours, or until the chickpeas are very tender.

4 Season with salt and pepper, then add the vermicelli or soup pasta to the pan and cook for 5–6 minutes until it is just tender. If the soup is very thick at this stage, add a little more water.

5 Beat the egg yolks with the lemon juice and stir into the simmering soup. Immediately remove the soup from the heat and stir until thickened. Pour into warmed serving bowls and garnish with plenty of fresh coriander. Serve the soup with lemon wedges.

COOK'S TIP
If you have forgotten to soak the chickpeas overnight, place them in a pan with about four times their volume of cold water. Bring very slowly to the boil, then cover the pan, remove it from the heat and leave to stand for 45 minutes before using as described in the recipe.

COURGETTE FRITTERS with PISTOU

A wide variety of different organic courgettes are available, ranging in colour from pale yellow to deep green. The pistou sauce, made with fresh basil, provides a lovely contrast in flavour, but you could substitute other sauces, such as a tomato and garlic one or a herb dressing.

SERVES FOUR

450g/1lb courgettes (zucchini), grated
75g/3oz/⅔ cup plain (all-purpose) or
    wholemeal (whole-wheat) flour
1 egg, separated
15ml/1 tbsp olive oil
oil for shallow frying
sea salt and ground black pepper

For the pistou sauce
15g/½oz/½ cup basil leaves
4 garlic cloves, crushed
90g/3½oz/1 cup finely grated
    Parmesan cheese or premium
    Italian-style vegetarian cheese
finely grated rind of 1 lemon
150ml/¼ pint/⅔ cup olive oil

1 To make the pistou sauce, crush the basil leaves and garlic in a mortar with a pestle to make a fine paste. Transfer the paste to a bowl and stir in the grated cheese and lemon rind. Gradually blend in the oil, a little at a time, until combined, then transfer to a serving dish.

2 To make the fritters, put the grated courgettes in a sieve over a bowl and sprinkle with plenty of salt. Leave for 1 hour then rinse thoroughly. Dry well on kitchen paper.

3 Sift the flour into a bowl and make a well in the centre, then add the egg yolk and oil. Measure 75ml/5 tbsp water and add a little to the bowl.

4 Whisk the egg yolk and oil, gradually incorporating the flour and water to make a smooth batter. Season and set aside for 30 minutes.

5 Stir the grated, rinsed courgettes into the batter. Whisk the egg white until stiff, then fold into the batter.

6 Heat 1cm/½in of oil in a frying pan. Add dessertspoons of batter to the oil and fry for about 2 minutes until golden brown and crispy. Remove from the pan, using a slotted spoon. Place the fritters on kitchen paper and keep warm while frying the rest. Serve the hot fritters with the pistou sauce.

GRILLED AUBERGINE PARCELS

This is a great organic recipe – little Italian bundles of tomatoes, mozzarella cheese and basil, wrapped in slices of aubergine. The parcels are naturally low in saturated fat, sugar and salt but are indulgent and delicious, too.

SERVES FOUR

2 large, long aubergines (eggplant)
225g/8oz buffalo mozzarella cheese
2 plum tomatoes
16 large basil leaves
30ml/2 tbsp olive oil
sea salt and ground black pepper

For the dressing
60ml/4 tbsp olive oil
5ml/1 tsp balsamic vinegar
15ml/1 tbsp sun-dried tomato purée (paste)
15ml/1 tbsp lemon juice

For the garnish
30ml/2 tbsp toasted pine nuts
torn basil leaves

1 Remove the stalks from the aubergines and then cut the aubergines lengthways into thin, even slices – the aim is to get 16 slices in total (each about 5mm/¼in thick), disregarding the first and last slices.

2 Bring a large pan of water to the boil and cook the aubergine slices for 2 minutes. Drain, then dry on kitchen paper.

3 Cut the mozzarella cheese into eight slices. Cut each tomato into eight slices, not counting the first and last slices.

4 Take two aubergine slices and place on a flameproof tray, in a cross. Place a slice of tomato in the centre, season lightly, add a basil leaf, then a slice of mozzarella, another basil leaf, a slice of tomato and more seasoning.

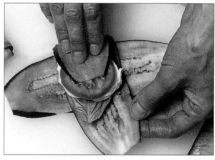

5 Fold the ends of the aubergine slices around the mozzarella and tomato filling to make a parcel. Repeat with the rest of the ingredients to make eight parcels. Chill the parcels for 20 minutes.

6 To make the tomato dressing, whisk together all the ingredients and season to taste with salt and pepper.

7 Preheat the grill (broiler). Brush the parcels with oil and cook for 5 minutes on each side. Serve hot, with the dressing, sprinkled with pine nuts and basil.

ROAST GARLIC with GOAT'S CHEESE PÂTÉ

*The combination of sweet, mellow roasted garlic and goat's cheese is a classic one. The pâté
is flavoured with walnuts and herbs and is particularly good made with the new season's
walnuts, sometimes known as "wet" walnuts, which are available in the early autumn.*

SERVES FOUR

4 large garlic bulbs
4 fresh rosemary sprigs
8 fresh thyme sprigs
60ml/4 tbsp olive oil
sea salt and ground black pepper
thyme sprigs, to garnish
4–8 slices sourdough bread and
   walnuts, to serve

For the pâté
200g/7oz/scant 1 cup soft goat's cheese
5ml/1 tsp finely chopped fresh thyme
15ml/1 tbsp chopped fresh parsley
50g/2oz/⅓ cup walnuts, chopped
15ml/1 tbsp walnut oil (optional)
fresh thyme, to garnish

1 Preheat the oven to 180°C/350°F/
Gas 4. Strip the papery skin from the
garlic bulbs. Place them in an ovenproof
dish large enough to hold them snugly.
Tuck in the fresh rosemary sprigs and
fresh thyme sprigs, drizzle the olive oil
over and season with a little sea salt and
plenty of ground black pepper.

2 Cover the garlic tightly with foil and
bake in the oven for 50–60 minutes,
opening the parcel and basting once
halfway through the cooking time. Set
aside and leave to cool.

3 Preheat the grill (broiler). To make
the pâté, cream the cheese with the
thyme, parsley and chopped walnuts.
Beat in 15ml/1 tbsp of the cooking oil
from the garlic and season to taste with
plenty of ground black pepper. Transfer
the pâté to a serving bowl and chill
until ready to serve.

4 Brush the sourdough bread slices on
one side with the remaining cooking oil
from the garlic bulbs, then grill (broil)
until lightly toasted.

5 Divide the pâté among four individual
plates. Drizzle the walnut oil, if using,
over the goat's cheese pâté and grind
some black pepper over it. Place some
garlic on each plate and serve with the
pâté and some toasted bread. Garnish
the pâté with a little fresh thyme and
serve a few freshly shelled walnuts
with each portion.

SLOW-COOKED SHIITAKE with SHOYU

Shiitake mushrooms cooked slowly are so rich and filling, that some people call them
"vegetarian steak". This Japanese dish, known as Fukumé-ni, can last a few weeks in
the refrigerator, and is a useful and flavourful addition to other dishes.

SERVES FOUR

20 dried shiitake mushrooms
45ml/3 tbsp sunflower or safflower oil
30ml/2 tbsp shoyu
15ml/1 tbsp toasted sesame oil

VARIATION
You can make a delicious rice dish using
the slow-cooked shiitake to serve with
grilled fish or chicken. Cut the slow-
cooked shiitake into thin strips. Mix with
600g/1lb 5oz/5¼ cups cooked brown rice
and 15ml/1 tbsp finely chopped chives.
Serve in individual rice bowls and sprinkle
with toasted sesame seeds.

1 Start soaking the dried shiitake the
day before. Put them in a large bowl
almost full of water. Cover the shiitake
with a plate or lid to stop them floating
to the surface of the water. Leave to
soak overnight.

2 Measure 120ml/4fl oz/½ cup liquid
from the bowl. Drain the shiitake into a
sieve. Remove and discard the stalks.

3 Heat the oil in a wok or a large frying
pan. Stir-fry the shiitake over a high heat
for 5 minutes, stirring continuously.

4 Reduce the heat to the lowest setting,
then add the measured liquid and the
shoyu. Cook the mushrooms until there
is almost no moisture left, stirring
frequently. Add the toasted sesame oil
and remove from the heat.

5 Leave to cool, then slice and arrange
the shiitake on a large plate.

SPICED ONION KOFTAS

These delicious Indian onion fritters are made with chickpea flour, otherwise known as gram flour or besan, which has a distinctive nutty flavour. Serve with chutney or a yogurt dip.

3 Add the chickpea flour and baking powder to the onion mixture in the bowl, then use your hand to mix all the ingredients thoroughly.

4 Shape the mixture by hand into 12–15 koftas about the size of golf balls.

5 Heat the sunflower oil for deep-frying to 180–190°C/350–375°F, or until a cube of day-old bread browns in about 30–45 seconds. Fry the koftas, four to five at a time, until deep golden brown all over. Remove with a slotted spoon and drain each batch on kitchen paper and keep warm until all the koftas are cooked. Serve the koftas warm with lemon wedges (if using), coriander sprigs and a yogurt and herb dip.

MAKES TWELVE TO FIFTEEN

675g/1½lb onions, halved and thinly sliced
5ml/1 tsp sea salt
5ml/1 tsp ground coriander
5ml/1 tsp ground cumin
2.5ml/½ tsp ground turmeric
1–2 green chillies, seeded and
    finely chopped
45ml/3 tbsp chopped fresh coriander
    (cilantro)
90g/3½oz/¾ cup chickpea flour
2.5ml/½ tsp baking powder
sunflower oil, for deep-frying

To serve
lemon wedges (optional)
fresh coriander sprigs
yogurt and herb dip (see Cook's Tip)

1 Place the onions in a colander, add the salt and toss. Place on a plate and leave to stand for 45 minutes, tossing once or twice. Rinse the onions, then squeeze out any excess moisture.

2 Place the onions in a bowl. Add the ground coriander, cumin, turmeric, finely chopped chillies and chopped fresh coriander. Mix well.

COOK'S TIP
To make a yogurt and herb dip to serve with the koftas, stir 30ml/2 tbsp each of chopped fresh coriander (cilantro) and mint into about 225g/8oz/1 cup set natural (plain) yogurt. Season with salt, ground toasted cumin seeds and a pinch of muscovado (brown) sugar.

LENTIL DHAL with ROASTED GARLIC

This spicy lentil dhal makes a sustaining and comforting meal when served with brown rice or Indian breads and any dry-spiced dish, particularly a cauliflower or potato dish.

SERVES FOUR TO SIX

40g/1½oz/3 tbsp butter or ghee
1 onion, chopped
2 green chillies, seeded and chopped
15ml/1 tbsp chopped fresh root ginger
225g/8oz/1 cup yellow or red lentils
900ml/1½ pints/3¾ cups water
45ml/3 tbsp roasted garlic purée (paste)
5ml/1 tsp ground cumin
5ml/1 tsp ground coriander
200g/7oz tomatoes, peeled and diced
a little lemon juice
sea salt and ground black pepper
30–45ml/2–3 tbsp coriander (cilantro)
   sprigs, to garnish

For the spicy garnish
30ml/2 tbsp sunflower oil
4–5 shallots, sliced
2 garlic cloves, thinly sliced
15g/½oz/1 tbsp butter or ghee
5ml/1 tsp cumin seeds
5ml/1 tsp mustard seeds
3–4 small dried red chillies
8–10 fresh curry leaves

1 First begin the spicy garnish. Heat the oil in a large, heavy pan. Add the shallots and fry them over a medium heat for 5–10 minutes, stirring occasionally, until they are crisp and browned. Add the garlic and cook, stirring frequently, for a moment or two until the garlic colours slightly. Remove the pan from the heat and use a slotted spoon to remove the shallots and garlic from the pan and set aside.

COOK'S TIP
Ghee is clarified butter that has had all the milk solids removed by heating – it was originally made to extend the keeping qualities of butter in India. It is the main cooking fat used in Indian cooking. Because the milk solids have been removed, ghee has a high smoking point and can therefore be cooked at higher temperatures than ordinary butter. Look for organic ghee in whole food stores.

2 Melt the 40g/1½oz/3 tbsp butter or ghee for the dhal in the pan, add the onion, chillies and ginger, and cook for 10 minutes until golden.

3 Stir in the yellow or red lentils and water, then bring to the boil, reduce the heat and part-cover the pan. Simmer, stirring occasionally, for 50–60 minutes until it is the same consistency as a very thick soup.

4 Stir in the roasted garlic purée, cumin and ground coriander, then season with salt and pepper to taste. Cook the dhal for a further 10–15 minutes, uncovered, stirring frequently.

5 Stir in the tomatoes and then adjust the seasoning, adding a little lemon juice to taste if necessary.

6 To finish the spicy garnish: melt the butter or ghee in a frying pan. Add the cumin and mustard seeds and fry until the mustard seeds begin to pop. Stir in the small dried red chillies and fresh curry leaves, then immediately swirl the mixture into the cooked dhal. Garnish with coriander and the spicy fried shallots and garlic and serve.

ASSORTED SEAWEED SALAD

This salad is a fine example of the traditional Japanese idea of eating: look after your appetite and your health at the same time. Seaweed is a nutritious, alkaline food which is rich in fibre. Its unusual flavours are a great complement to fish and tofu dishes.

SERVES FOUR

5g/⅛oz each dried wakame, dried arame
   and dried hijiki seaweeds
about 130g/4½oz enokitake mushrooms
2 spring onions (scallions)
a few ice cubes
½ cucumber, cut lengthways
250g/9oz mixed salad leaves

For the marinade
15ml/1 tbsp rice vinegar
6.5ml/1¼ tsp salt

For the dressing
60ml/4 tbsp rice vinegar
7.5ml/1½ tsp toasted sesame oil
15ml/1 tbsp shoyu
15ml/1 tbsp water with a pinch
   of dashi-no-moto (dashi
   stock granules)
2.5cm/1in piece fresh root ginger,
   finely grated

1 First rehydrate the seaweeds. Soak the dried wakame seaweed for 10 minutes in one bowl of water and, in a separate bowl of water, soak the dried arame and hijiki seaweeds together for 30 minutes.

2 Trim the hard end of the enokitake mushroom stalks, then cut the bunch in half and separate the stems.

3 Slice the spring onions into thin, 4cm/1½in long strips, then soak the strips in a bowl of cold water with a few ice cubes added to make them curl up. Drain. Slice the cucumber into thin, half-moon shapes.

4 Cook the wakame and enokitake in boiling water for 2 minutes, then add the arame and hijiki for a few seconds. Immediately remove from the heat. Drain and sprinkle over the vinegar and salt while still warm. Chill until needed.

5 Mix the dressing ingredients in a bowl. Arrange the mixed salad leaves in a large bowl with the cucumber on top, then add the seaweed and enokitake mixture. Decorate the salad with spring onion curls and serve with the dressing.

MARINATED SALMON with AVOCADO SALAD

Use only the freshest of salmon for this delicious salad. The marinade of lemon juice and
dashi-konbu "cooks" the salmon, which is then served with avocado, toasted almonds
and salad leaves, accompanied by a miso mayonnaise.

SERVES FOUR

2 very fresh salmon tails, skinned and
    filleted, 250g/9oz total weight
juice of 1 lemon
10cm/4in dashi-konbu seaweed, wiped with
    a damp cloth and cut into 4 strips
1 ripe avocado
4 shiso or basil leaves, stalks removed and
    cut in half lengthways
about 115g/4oz mixed leaves such as
    lamb's lettuce, frisée or rocket (arugula)
45ml/3 tbsp flaked (sliced) almonds,
    toasted in a dry frying pan until
    just slightly browned

For the miso mayonnaise
90ml/6 tbsp good-quality mayonnaise
15ml/1 tbsp miso paste
ground black pepper

1 Cut the first salmon fillet in half
crossways at the tail end where the fillet
is not wider than 4cm/1½in. Next, cut
the wider part in half lengthways. This
means the fillet from one side is cut into
three. Cut the other fillet into three
pieces, in the same way.

2 Pour the lemon juice into a wide,
shallow plastic container and add two of
the dashi-konbu pieces. Lay the salmon
fillets in the base of the container and
sprinkle with the rest of the dashi-konbu.
Marinate for about 15 minutes, then
turn the salmon and leave for a further
15 minutes. The salmon should change
to a pink "cooked" colour. Remove the
salmon from the marinade and wipe
with kitchen paper.

3 Holding a very sharp knife at an angle,
cut the salmon into 5mm/¼in thick slices
against the grain.

4 Halve the avocado and sprinkle with a
little of the remaining salmon marinade.
Remove the avocado stone (pit) and
skin, then carefully slice to the same
thickness as the salmon.

5 Mix the miso mayonnaise ingredients
in a small bowl. Spread about 5ml/1 tsp
on to the back of each of the shiso or
basil leaves, then mix the remainder with
15ml/1 tbsp of the remaining marinade
to loosen the mayonnaise.

6 Arrange the salad leaves on four
plates. Add the avocado, salmon, shiso
leaves and almonds and toss lightly.
Drizzle over the remaining mayonnaise
and serve immediately.

VARIATION
Alternatively, build a tower of avocado
and salmon. For each serving, place an
eighth of the avocado slices in the
centre of a plate, slightly overlapping.
Add a shiso or basil leaf, miso-side down.
Then place an eighth of the salmon
on top, slightly overlapping. Repeat
the process. Arrange the salad and
almonds, and spoon over the mayonnaise.

MAIN COURSES

When you cook organic ingredients with care – and flair – you rapidly develop a reputation for the quality of your food. To guarantee continued success serve something like Hake au Poivre, which allows the full flavour of the fish to shine while adding interest with a peppercorn crust and tangy red pepper relish. Give seafood the tender treatment by folding it into a creamy sauce and bedding it between sheets of fresh lasagne. Grilled Skewered Chicken is another winner. The outside of the poultry has a wonderful, almost toffee-like taste, which enhances but does not mask the excellent flavour of organic chicken.

MOROCCAN FISH TAGINE with COUSCOUS

Fish is a staple food for the organic cook, with its balance of amino acids and oils. Always ensure that it is either organically farmed or sustainably caught in the wild.

SERVES EIGHT

1.3kg/3lb firm fish fillets such as monkfish or
    hoki, skinned and cut into 5cm/2in cubes
60ml/4 tbsp olive oil
4 onions, chopped
1 large aubergine (eggplant), cut into
    1cm/½in cubes
2 courgettes (zucchini), cut into
    1cm/½in cubes
400g/14oz can chopped tomatoes
400ml/14fl oz/1⅔ cups passata (bottled
    strained tomatoes)
200ml/7fl oz/scant 1 cup fish stock
1 preserved lemon, chopped
90g/3½oz/scant 1 cup olives
60ml/4 tbsp chopped fresh coriander (cilantro)
sea salt and ground black pepper
couscous, to serve
coriander sprigs, to garnish

For the harissa
3 large fresh red chillies, seeded and chopped
3 garlic cloves, peeled
15ml/1 tbsp ground coriander
30ml/2 tbsp ground cumin
5ml/1 tsp ground cinnamon
grated rind of 1 lemon
30ml/2 tbsp sunflower oil

1 To make the harissa, whizz everything in a food processor to a smooth paste.

2 Put the fish in a wide bowl and add 30ml/2 tbsp of the harissa. Toss to coat, cover and chill for at least 1 hour.

3 Heat half the oil in a shallow pan. Cook the onions for about 10 minutes. Stir in the remaining harissa; cook for 5 minutes, stirring occasionally.

4 Heat the remaining olive oil in a separate pan. Add the aubergine cubes and fry for 10 minutes, or until they are golden brown. Add the cubed courgettes and fry the vegetables for a further 2 minutes, stirring occasionally.

5 Tip the aubergine mixture into the shallow pan and combine with the onions, then stir in the chopped tomatoes, the passata and fish stock. Bring to the boil, then lower the heat and simmer the mixture for about 20 minutes.

6 Stir the fish cubes and preserved lemon into the pan. Add the olives and stir gently. Cover and simmer over a low heat for about 15–20 minutes until the fish is just cooked through. Season to taste. Stir in the chopped coriander. Serve with couscous and garnish with coriander sprigs.

COOK'S TIP
To make the fish go further, you could add 225g/8oz/1¼ cups cooked chickpeas to the tagine.

HAKE AU POIVRE with RED PEPPER RELISH

Use South African hake rather than hake from European waters, where stocks are low due
to overfishing. Or try line-caught tuna or haddock from Icelandic waters.

3 Make the relish. Cut the red peppers in half lengthways, remove the core and seeds from each and cut the flesh into 1cm/½in wide strips. Heat the olive oil in a wok or a shallow pan that has a lid. Add the peppers and stir them for about 5 minutes, or until they are slightly softened. Stir in the chopped garlic, tomatoes and the anchovies, then cover the pan and simmer the mixture very gently for about 20 minutes, until the peppers are very soft.

4 Tip the contents of the pan into a food processor and whizz to a coarse purée. Transfer to a bowl and season to taste. Stir in the capers, balsamic vinegar and basil. Keep the relish hot.

SERVES FOUR

30–45ml/2–3 tbsp mixed peppercorns
  (black, white, pink and green)
4 hake steaks, about 175g/6oz each
30ml/2 tbsp olive oil
sea salt and ground black pepper

For the relish
2 red (bell) peppers
15ml/1 tbsp olive oil
2 garlic cloves, chopped
4 ripe tomatoes, peeled, seeded
  and quartered
4 drained canned anchovy fillets,
  roughly chopped
5ml/1 tsp capers
15ml/1 tbsp balsamic vinegar,
  plus a little extra to serve
12 fresh basil leaves, shredded, plus
  a few extra to garnish

1 Put the peppercorns in a mortar and crush them coarsely with a pestle. Alternatively, put them in a plastic bag and crush them with a rolling pin.

2 Season the hake fillets lightly with salt, then coat them evenly on both sides with the crushed peppercorns. Set the coated fish steaks aside while you make the red pepper relish.

5 Heat the olive oil in a shallow pan, add the hake steaks and fry them, in batches if necessary, for 5 minutes on each side, turning them once or twice, until they are just cooked through.

6 Place the fish on individual plates and spoon a little red pepper relish on to each plate. Garnish with basil leaves and a little extra balsamic vinegar. Serve the rest of the relish separately.

SEAFOOD LASAGNE

This dish can be as simple or as elegant as you like. For an elegant dinner party, you can dress it up with scallops, mussels or prawns; for a casual family supper, you can use simple fish such as haddock and hoki. Whatever fish or shellfish you choose, ensure it comes from a sustainable source.

SERVES EIGHT

350g/12oz haddock
350g/12oz salmon fillet
350g/12oz undyed smoked haddock
1 litre/1¾ pints/4 cups milk or
   soya milk
500ml/17fl oz/2¼ cups fish stock
2 bay leaves
1 small onion, peeled and halved
75g/3oz/6 tbsp butter or
   non-hydrogenated margarine,
   plus extra for greasing
45ml/3 tbsp plain (all-purpose) or
   wholemeal (whole-wheat) flour
150g/5oz/2 cups mushrooms, sliced
225–300g/8–11oz fresh lasagne
60ml/4 tbsp freshly grated Parmesan
   cheese or premium Italian-style
   vegetarian cheese
sea salt, ground black pepper, freshly
   grated nutmeg and paprika
rocket (arugula) leaves, to garnish

For the tomato sauce
30ml/2 tbsp olive oil
1 red onion, finely chopped
1 garlic clove, finely chopped
400g/14oz can chopped tomatoes
15ml/1 tbsp tomato purée (paste)
15ml/1 tbsp torn fresh basil leaves

1 Make the tomato sauce. Heat the oil in a pan and fry the onion and garlic over a low heat for 5 minutes, until softened and golden. Stir in the tomatoes and tomato purée and simmer for 20–30 minutes, stirring occasionally. Season with a little salt and plenty of black pepper and stir in the basil.

VARIATION
A good selection of organic pastas are available, including a variety of types of lasagne. Choose from classic lasagne, lasagne all'uovo (rich egg pasta sheets) or lasagne verdi (spinach lasagne), which is an attractive dark green colour.

2 Put all the fish in a shallow flameproof dish or pan with the milk, stock, bay leaves and onion. Bring to the boil over a moderate heat; poach for 5 minutes, until almost cooked. Leave to cool.

3 When the fish is almost cold, strain it, reserving the liquid. Remove the skin and any bones, and flake the fish.

4 Preheat the oven to 180°C/350°F/ Gas 4. Melt the butter in a pan, stir in the flour; cook for 2 minutes, stirring. Gradually add the poaching liquid and bring to the boil, stirring. Add the mushrooms and cook for 2–3 minutes. Season with salt, pepper and nutmeg.

5 Lightly grease a shallow rectangular ovenproof dish. Spoon a thin layer of the mushroom sauce over the base of the dish and spread it out evenly with a spatula. Stir the flaked fish into the remaining mushroom sauce in the pan.

6 Add a layer of lasagne, then a layer of fish and sauce. Add another layer of lasagne, then spread over all the tomato sauce. Continue to layer the lasagne and fish, finishing with a layer of fish.

7 Sprinkle over the grated cheese, then bake for 30–45 minutes until golden. Before serving, sprinkle with paprika and garnish with rocket leaves.

PROVENÇAL AIOLI with SMOKED HADDOCK

This substantial salad is a meal on its own and perfect for summer entertaining. Choose organic vegetables and vary them according to what is in season as the summer progresses.

SERVES SIX

1kg/2¼lb smoked haddock
bouquet garni
18 small new potatoes, scrubbed
1 large or 2 small fresh mint sprigs, torn
225g/8oz French (green) beans, trimmed
225g/8oz broccoli florets
6 eggs, hard-boiled
12 baby carrots, with leaves if possible,
    scrubbed
1 large red (bell) pepper, seeded and cut
    into strips
2 fennel bulbs, cut into strips
18 red or yellow cherry tomatoes
sea salt
6 large whole cooked prawns (shrimp)
    or langoustines, in the shell,
    to garnish (optional)

For the aioli
600ml/1 pint/2½ cups home-made or
    good-quality bought mayonnaise
2 fat garlic cloves (or more if you
    prefer), crushed
cayenne pepper

1 Put the smoked haddock into a sauté pan and pour in enough water to barely cover the fish. Add the bouquet garni. Bring the water to the boil, then cover and poach very gently for about 10 minutes until the fish flakes quite easily when tested with the tip of a sharp knife. Drain the fish, discard the bouquet garni and set aside until required.

2 Cook the potatoes with the mint in a pan of lightly salted boiling water until just tender. Drain and set aside.

3 Cook the beans and broccoli in separate pans of lightly salted boiling water for about 5 minutes. They should still be very crisp. Refresh the vegetables under cold water and drain again, then set aside.

4 Remove the skin from the haddock and break the flesh into large flakes. Shell the eggs and halve them lengthways.

5 Pile the haddock in the middle of a large serving platter and arrange the eggs and all the vegetables round the edges or randomly. Garnish with the prawns or langoustines if you are using them.

6 To make the aioli, put the mayonnaise in a bowl and stir in the crushed garlic and cayenne pepper to taste. Serve in individual bowls or one large bowl to hand round.

GRILLED SKEWERED CHICKEN

Organic chicken has a superb flavour and these fabulous little skewers make great finger food. Cook on the barbecue or grill and serve sizzling hot.

SERVES FOUR

8 chicken thighs with skin, boned
8 large, thick spring onions (scallions),
   trimmed
oil, for greasing
lemon wedges, to serve

For the yakitori sauce
60ml/4 tbsp sake
75ml/5 tbsp shoyu
15ml/1 tbsp mirin
15ml/1 tbsp unrefined caster (superfine)
   sugar or rapadura

1 First, make the *yakitori* sauce. Mix all the ingredients together in a small pan. Bring to the boil, then reduce the heat and simmer for 10 minutes.

2 Cut the chicken into 2.5cm/1in cubes. Cut the spring onions into 2.5cm/1in long sticks.

3 To cook the chicken on a barbecue, soak eight bamboo skewers overnight in water. This prevents the skewers from burning during cooking. Prepare the barbecue. Thread about four pieces of chicken and three spring onion pieces on to each of the skewers. Place the *yakitori* sauce in a small bowl and have a brush ready.

4 Cook the skewered chicken on the barbecue. Keep the skewer handles away from the fire, turning them frequently. Brush the chicken with sauce. Return to the coals and repeat this process twice more until the chicken is well cooked.

5 Alternatively, to grill (broil), preheat the grill (broiler) to high. Oil the wire rack and spread out the chicken cubes on it. Grill both sides of the chicken until the juices drip, then dip the pieces in the sauce and put back on the rack. Grill for 30 seconds on each side, repeating the dipping process twice more.

6 Set aside and keep warm. Gently grill the spring onions until soft and slightly brown outside. Do not dip. Thread the chicken and spring onion pieces on to skewers as above.

7 Arrange the skewered chicken and spring onions on a serving platter and serve accompanied by lemon wedges.

SPAGHETTI with EGGS and BACON

Organic ingredients really enhance the flavours of simple, classic dishes such as this Italian favourite, which makes a great last-minute supper.

SERVES FOUR

30ml/2 tbsp olive oil
1 small onion, finely chopped
1 large garlic clove, crushed
8 pancetta or rindless smoked streaky (fatty) bacon rashers (strips), cut into 1cm/½in strips
350g/12oz fresh or dried spaghetti
4 eggs
90–120ml/6–8 tbsp reduced-fat crème fraîche
60ml/4 tbsp freshly grated Parmesan cheese or premium Italian-style vegetarian cheese, plus extra to serve
sea salt and ground black pepper

1 Heat the oil in a large pan, add the onion and garlic and fry gently for about 5 minutes until softened.

2 Add the pancetta or bacon to the pan and cook for 10 minutes, stirring.

3 Meanwhile, cook the spaghetti in a large pan of salted boiling water for 10 minutes or according to the instructions on the packet until *al dente*.

4 Put the eggs, crème fraîche and grated Parmesan in a bowl. Stir in plenty of black pepper, then beat together well.

5 Drain the pasta thoroughly, tip it into the pan with the pancetta or bacon and toss well to mix.

6 Turn off the heat under the pan, then immediately add the egg mixture and toss thoroughly so that it cooks lightly and coats the pasta.

7 Season to taste, then divide the spaghetti among four warmed bowls and sprinkle with freshly ground black pepper. Serve immediately, with extra grated cheese handed separately.

COOK'S TIP
You can replace the crème fraîche with double (heavy) cream, sour cream or soya cream, if you prefer.

CHICKEN with CASHEW NUTS

This popular Chinese dish is quick and easy to make and can be enjoyed to the full by using good-quality organic products that are full of flavour.

SERVES FOUR

350g/12oz skinless chicken
   breast fillets
pinch of ground white pepper
15ml/1 tbsp dry sherry
300ml/½ pint/1¼ cups chicken stock
15ml/1 tbsp sunflower oil
1 garlic clove, finely chopped
1 small carrot, cut into cubes
½ cucumber, about 75g/3oz, cut into
   1cm/½in cubes
50g/2oz/½ cup drained canned bamboo
   shoots, cut into 1cm/½in cubes
   (optional)
5ml/1 tsp cornflour (cornstarch)
15ml/1 tbsp soy sauce
25g/1oz/¼ cup dry-roasted cashew nuts
2.5ml/½ tsp sesame oil
noodles, to serve

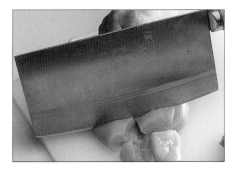

1 Cut the chicken into 2cm/¾in cubes. Place the cubes in a bowl, stir in the white pepper and sherry, cover and marinate for 15 minutes.

2 Bring the stock to the boil in a large pan. Add the chicken and cook, stirring, for 3 minutes. Drain, reserving 90ml/ 6 tbsp of the stock, and set aside.

3 Heat the sunflower oil in a large non-stick frying pan until it is very hot, add the finely chopped garlic and stir-fry for a few seconds. Add the cubed carrot, cucumber and bamboo shoots, if using, and continue to stir-fry the vegetables over a medium heat for 2 minutes.

4 Stir in the chicken and reserved stock. Mix the cornflour with the soy sauce and add the mixture to the pan. Cook, stirring, until the sauce thickens slightly. Finally, add the cashew nuts and sesame oil. Toss to mix thoroughly, then serve with noodles.

LAMB STEW with NEW POTATOES and SHALLOTS

This fresh lemon-seasoned stew is finished with an Italian mixture of chopped garlic,
parsley and lemon rind known as gremolata, the traditional topping for osso bucco.

SERVES SIX

1kg/2¼lb boneless shoulder of lamb,
    trimmed of fat and cut into
    5cm/2in cubes
1 garlic clove, finely chopped
finely grated rind of ½ lemon and
    juice of 1 lemon
90ml/6 tbsp olive oil
45ml/3 tbsp wholemeal (whole-wheat) flour
1 large onion, sliced
5 anchovy fillets in olive oil, drained
2.5ml/½ tsp unrefined caster (superfine)
    sugar or rapadura
300ml/½ pint/1¼ cups fruity white wine
475ml/16fl oz/2 cups lamb stock or half
    stock and half water
1 fresh bay leaf
fresh rosemary sprig
fresh parsley sprig
500g/1¼lb small new potatoes
250g/9oz shallots, peeled but left whole
45ml/3 tbsp double (heavy) cream or
    soya cream (optional)
sea salt and ground black pepper

For the gremolata
1 garlic clove, finely chopped
finely shredded rind of ½ lemon
45ml/3 tbsp chopped fresh flat leaf parsley

1 Mix the lamb with the garlic and the rind and juice of ½ lemon in a non-metallic container. Season with pepper and mix in 15ml/1 tbsp olive oil, then leave to marinate in the refrigerator for 12–24 hours.

2 Drain the lamb carefully, reserving the marinade, and pat the lamb dry with kitchen paper. Preheat the oven to 180°C/350°F/Gas 4.

COOK'S TIP
A mezzaluna (double-handled, half-moon shaped, curved chopping blade) makes a very good job of chopping gremolata ingredients. If using a food processor or electric chopper, take care not to over-process the mixture as it is easy to mince the ingredients to a paste.

3 Heat 30ml/2 tbsp olive oil in a large, heavy frying pan. Season the flour with salt and pepper and toss the drained, dried lamb in it to coat it lightly, shaking off any excess flour. Add the lamb to the pan, in small batches, and seal it on all sides in the hot oil stirring constantly with a wooden spoon.

4 As each batch of lamb becomes brown, transfer it to an ovenproof pan or flame-proof casserole. You may need to add an extra 15ml/1 tbsp olive oil to the pan.

5 Reduce the heat, add another 15ml/1 tbsp oil to the pan and cook the sliced onion gently over a very low heat, stirring frequently, for 10 minutes until softened and golden but not browned. Add the drained anchovy fillets and the sugar, and cook, mashing the anchovies into the onion with a wooden spoon.

6 Add the reserved marinade, increase the heat a little and cook for 1–2 minutes, then pour in the fruity white wine and lamb stock or lamb stock and water, and bring to the boil. Simmer the sauce gently for about 5 minutes, then pour the sauce over the lamb in the pan or casserole.

7 Tie the bay leaf, rosemary and parsley together to make a bouquet garni and add to the lamb. Season the stew, then cover tightly and cook in the oven for 1 hour. Add the potatoes to the stew and stir well, then return the stew to the oven and cook for a further 20 minutes.

8 Meanwhile, to make the gremolata, chop the garlic, lemon rind and parsley together finely. Place in a dish, then cover and set aside.

9 Heat the remaining olive oil in a frying pan and brown the shallots on all sides, then stir them into the lamb stew. Cover and cook the stew for a further 30–40 minutes until the lamb is tender. Transfer the lamb and vegetables to a warmed serving dish and keep hot. Discard the bunch of herbs.

10 Boil the remaining cooking juices to reduce, then add the double cream or soya cream, if using, and simmer for 2–3 minutes. Adjust the seasoning, adding a little lemon juice to taste if liked. Pour this sauce over the lamb, scatter the gremolata mixture over the top and serve immediately.

DESSERTS

Just because you care about where your food comes from, it doesn't mean you've committed yourself to a life of self-denial. Choosing to eat organic means more, not less, of the good things in life, such as exquisitely flavoured figs with hazelnut ice cream or citrus custards topped with a crunchy layer of caramel. Spoil yourself with Chocolate Meringues with Mixed Fruit Compote or try the scrumptious Chocolate Mousse with Glazed Kumquats. Berry fruits warmed in honey and fruit juice are the perfect accompaniment for the meringues, and because organic chocolate is actually good for you in small doses, you can indulge without too much guilt.

HONEY BAKED FIGS with HAZELNUT ICE CREAM

Organic figs have a deliciously intense flavour. They are smaller than non-organic fruit as they are not forced to absorb water during growing, so you may need three per person.

SERVES FOUR

1 lemon grass stalk, finely chopped
1 cinnamon stick, roughly broken
60ml/4 tbsp clear honey
200ml/7fl oz/scant 1 cup water
8 large or 12 small figs

For the hazelnut ice cream
450ml/¾ pint/scant 2 cups double (heavy) cream or soya cream
50g/2oz/¼ cup unrefined caster (superfine) sugar or rapadura
3 egg yolks
1.5ml/¼ tsp vanilla essence (extract)
75g/3oz/¾ cup hazelnuts

1 To make the ice cream, place the cream in a pan and heat slowly until almost boiling. Place the sugar and egg yolks in a bowl and whisk until creamy.

2 Pour a little cream on to the egg yolk mixture and stir. Pour into the pan and mix with the rest of the cream. Cook over a low heat, stirring constantly, until the mixture lightly coats the back of the spoon – do not allow it to boil. Pour into a bowl, stir in the vanilla and leave to cool.

3 Preheat the oven to 180°C/350°F/ Gas 4. Place the hazelnuts on a baking sheet and roast for 10–12 minutes, or until they are golden brown. Leave the nuts to cool, then place them in a food processor or blender and process until they are coarsely ground.

4 Transfer the ice cream mixture to a metal or plastic freezer container and freeze for 2 hours, or until the mixture feels firm around the edge. Remove the container from the freezer and whisk the ice cream to break down the ice crystals. Stir in the ground hazelnuts and freeze the mixture again until half-frozen. Whisk again, then freeze until firm.

COOK'S TIPS
• If you prefer, rather than whisking the semi-frozen ice cream, tip it into a food processor and process until smooth.
• There are several different types of organic figs available and they can all be used in this recipe. Choose from green-skinned figs that have an amber-coloured flesh, dark purple-skinned fruit with a deep red flesh or green/yellow-skinned figs with a pinky-coloured flesh.

5 Place the lemon grass, cinnamon stick, honey and water in a small pan and heat slowly until boiling. Simmer the mixture for 5 minutes, then leave the syrup to stand for 15 minutes.

6 Preheat the oven to 200°C/400°F/ Gas 6. Meanwhile, carefully cut the figs into quarters, leaving them intact at the bases. Place the figs in an ovenproof baking dish and pour over the honey-flavoured syrup.

7 Cover the dish tightly with foil and bake the figs for about 15 minutes, or until tender.

8 Take the ice cream from the freezer about 10 minutes before serving, to soften slightly. Transfer the figs to serving plates. Strain a little of the cooking liquid over the figs and then serve them with a scoop or two of hazelnut ice cream.

VARIATION
This recipe also works well with halved, stoned organic nectarines or peaches – cook as from step 6 and serve with the home-made ice cream.

SPICY PUMPKIN and ORANGE BOMBE

In this fabulous ice cream dessert, the subtle flavour of organic pumpkin is transformed with the addition of citrus fruits and spices. The delicious ice cream mixture is then encased in syrupy sponge and served with an orange and whole-spice syrup.

SERVES EIGHT

115g/4oz/½ cup unsalted (sweet) butter or
   non-hydrogenated margarine, softened
115g/4oz/generous ½ cup unrefined caster
   (superfine) sugar or rapadura
115g/4oz/1 cup self-raising
   (self-rising) flour
2.5ml/½ tsp baking powder
2 eggs

For the ice cream
450g/1lb fresh pumpkin, seeded and cubed
1 orange
300g/11oz/scant 1½ cups unrefined
   granulated sugar or rapadura
300ml/½ pint /1¼ cups water
2 cinnamon sticks, halved
10ml/2 tsp whole cloves
30ml/2 tbsp orange flower water
300ml/½ pint/1¼ cups extra thick double
   (heavy) cream or soya cream
2 pieces preserved stem ginger, grated
unrefined icing (confectioners') sugar,
   for dusting

1 Preheat the oven to 180°C/350°F/
Gas 4. Grease and base-line a 450g/1lb
loaf tin (pan).

2 To make the sponge, beat the butter
or margarine, caster sugar, flour, baking
powder and eggs in a bowl until creamy.

3 Spoon the mixture into the prepared
tin, then level the surface and bake in
the preheated oven for 30–35 minutes
until firm in the centre. Leave in the tin
for a few minutes then turn out on to a
wire rack to cool.

4 Make the ice cream. Steam the cubes
of pumpkin for about 15 minutes, or
until tender. Drain and blend in a food
processor to form a smooth purée.
Leave to cool.

5 Pare thin strips of rind from the
orange, scrape off any white pith, then
cut the strips into very fine shreds.
Squeeze the orange and set the juice
aside. Heat the unrefined sugar and water
in a small, heavy pan until the sugar
dissolves. Bring the syrup to the boil and
boil rapidly without stirring for 3 minutes.

6 Stir in the orange shreds, orange juice,
cinnamon and cloves and heat gently for
5 minutes. Strain the syrup, reserving
the orange shreds and spices. Measure
300ml/½ pint/1¼ cups of the syrup
and reserve. Return the spices to the
remaining syrup and stir in the orange
flower water. Pour into a jug (pitcher)
and set aside to cool.

COOK'S TIP
If you prefer a smooth syrup, strain to
remove the cinnamon sticks and cloves
before spooning it over the bombe.

7 Beat the pumpkin purée with 175ml/
6fl oz/¾ cup of the measured strained
syrup until evenly combined. Stir in the
cream and ginger. Cut the cake into 1cm/
½in slices. Dampen a 1.5 litre/2½ pint/
6¼ cup deep bowl and line it with clear
film (plastic wrap). Pour the remaining
strained syrup into a shallow dish.

8 Dip the cake slices one at a time
briefly in the syrup and use to line the
prepared bowl, placing the syrupy
coated sides against the bowl.

9 To freeze the ice cream by hand, pour
the pumpkin mixture into a shallow
container and freeze until firm. Scrape
the ice cream into the sponge-lined bowl,
level the surface and freeze until firm,
preferably overnight. If using an ice cream
maker, churn the pumpkin mixture until
very thick, then spoon it into the
sponge-lined bowl. Level the surface and
freeze until firm, preferably overnight.

10 To serve, invert the bombe on to a
plate. Lift off the bowl and clear film.
Dust with the icing sugar and serve
with the spiced syrup spooned over.

CHOCOLATE MERINGUES with MIXED FRUIT COMPOTE

Mini-chocolate meringues are sandwiched with crème fraîche and served with a compote of mixed summer berries to make this impressive dessert.

SERVES SIX

105ml/7 tbsp unsweetened red
   grape juice
105ml/7 tbsp unsweetened apple juice
30ml/2 tbsp clear honey
450g/1lb/4 cups mixed fresh summer
   berries, such as blackcurrants, redcurrants, raspberries and blackberries

For the meringues
3 egg whites
175g/6oz/¾ cup unrefined caster
   (superfine) sugar or rapadura
75g/3oz good-quality plain chocolate,
   finely grated
175g/6oz/scant 1 cup crème fraîche

1 Preheat the oven to 110°C/225°F/ Gas ¼. Grease and line two large baking sheets with baking parchment, cutting the paper to fit.

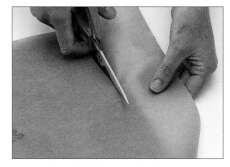

2 To make the meringues, whisk the egg whites in a large mixing bowl until stiff. Gradually whisk in half the sugar, then fold in the remaining sugar, using a metal spoon. Gently fold in the grated plain chocolate.

3 Carefully spoon the meringue mixture into a large piping (pastry) bag fitted with a large star nozzle. Pipe small round whirls of the mixture on to the prepared baking sheets.

4 Bake the meringues for 2½–3 hours until they are firm and crisp. Remove from the oven. Carefully peel the meringues off the paper, then transfer them to a wire rack to cool.

5 Meanwhile, make the compote. Heat the fruit juices in a small pan with the honey until almost boiling.

COOK'S TIP
Organic chocolate has a slightly higher proportion of cocoa and less sugar than non-organic equivalents. And, as organic cocoa is naturally high in tannins and antioxidant flavonoids as well as B vitamins and iron, organic chocolate consumed in moderation is actually good for you. Look for chocolate that has 70 per cent cocoa solids for the best flavour and higher nutritional content.

6 Place the mixed fresh berries in a large bowl and pour over the hot fruit juice and honey mixture. Stir gently to mix, then set aside and leave to cool. Once cool, cover the bowl with clear film (plastic wrap) and chill until required.

7 When ready to serve, gently sandwich the cold meringues together with the crème fraîche and arrange them on a serving plate or dish.

8 Serve the meringues immediately on individual plates with the mixed fruit compote to accompany.

VARIATION
Packs of frozen mixed berries are available and can be used in place of fresh in this recipe. Allow the berries to defrost thoroughly in a sieve over a mixing bowl, then use as in step 6.

CITRUS and CARAMEL CUSTARDS

Make these Spanish-style custards with organic milk as it is the only type of milk guaranteed to be free of GMOs and excess added antibiotics and hormones. Wonderfully smooth, the custards are delicately scented with tangy citrus flavours and aromatic cinnamon.

SERVES FOUR

450ml/³⁄₄ pint/scant 2 cups milk or soya milk
150ml/¹⁄₄ pint/²⁄₃ cup single (light) cream
   or soya cream
1 cinnamon stick, broken in half
thinly pared rind of ½ lemon
thinly pared rind of ½ orange
4 egg yolks
5ml/1 tsp cornflour (cornstarch)
40g/1½oz/3 tbsp unrefined caster
   (superfine) sugar or rapadura
grated rind of ½ lemon
grated rind of ½ orange
unrefined icing (confectioner's) sugar,
   to dust

1 Place the milk and cream in a pan. Add the cinnamon stick halves and the strips of pared lemon and orange rind. Bring to the boil, then reduce the heat and simmer for 10 minutes.

2 Preheat the oven to 160°C/325°F/Gas 3. Whisk the egg yolks, cornflour and sugar together. Remove the rinds and cinnamon from the hot milk and cream and discard. Whisk the hot milk and cream into the egg yolk mixture.

3 Add the grated citrus rind to the custard mixture and stir through. Pour into four individual dishes, each 13cm/5in in diameter. Place in a roasting pan and pour warm water into the pan to reach three-quarters of the way up the sides. Bake for 25 minutes, or until the custards are just set. Remove the dishes from the water; leave to cool, then chill.

4 Preheat the grill (broiler) to high. Sprinkle the custards liberally with icing sugar and place under the grill until the tops turn golden brown and caramelize.

COOK'S TIPS
• Prepare the grated rind first, then cut a few strips of rind from the ungrated side using a swivel-bladed vegetable peeler.
• You can use a special cook's blowtorch or salamander to caramelize the tops instead of grilling (broiling) them.

CHOCOLATE MOUSSE with GLAZED KUMQUATS

Bright orange kumquats balance this rich, dark mousse perfectly. There are some excellent organic chocolates available. It is worth spending a little more on them because they have such a luxurious taste and texture, and good fair-trade values.

SERVES SIX

225g/8oz dark (bittersweet) chocolate, broken into squares
4 eggs, separated
30ml/2 tbsp brandy
90ml/6 tbsp double (heavy) cream or soya cream

For the glazed kumquats
275g/10oz kumquats
115g/4oz/generous ½ cup unrefined granulated sugar or rapadura
150ml/¼ pint/⅔ cup water
15ml/1 tbsp brandy

1 Make the glazed kumquats. Slice the fruit lengthways and place cut side up in a shallow serving dish.

2 Place the sugar in a pan with the water. Heat gently, stirring constantly, until the sugar has dissolved, then bring to the boil and boil rapidly, without stirring, until a golden-brown caramel forms.

VARIATION
If you can't find kumquats, then use peeled and sliced small, seedless organic oranges, pink-fleshed grapefruit or satsumas instead.

3 Remove the pan from the heat and very carefully stir in 60ml/4 tbsp boiling water to dissolve the caramel. Stir in the brandy, then pour the caramel over the kumquats and leave to cool. Once completely cold, cover and chill.

4 Line a shallow 20cm/8in round cake tin (pan) with clear film (plastic wrap). Melt the chocolate in a bowl over a pan of barely simmering water, then remove the bowl from the heat.

5 Add the egg yolks and brandy to the chocolate and beat well, then fold in the cream, mixing well. In a separate clean bowl, whisk the egg whites until stiff, then gently fold them into the chocolate mixture.

6 Pour the mixture into the prepared tin and level the surface with a spatula. Chill for several hours until set.

7 To serve, turn the mousse out on to a plate and cut into slices or wedges. Serve the chocolate mousse on serving plates and spoon some of the glazed kumquats and syrup alongside.

CHRISTMAS ICE CREAM TORTE

This fruity ice cream cake makes an exciting alternative to traditional Christmas pudding, but don't feel that you have to limit it to the festive season. Packed with dried organic fruit and nuts, it is perfect for any special occasion and tastes sensational.

SERVES EIGHT TO TEN

75g/3oz/¾ cup dried cranberries
75g/3oz/scant ½ cup pitted prunes
50g/2oz/⅓ cup sultanas (golden raisins)
175ml/6fl oz/¾ cup port
2 pieces preserved stem ginger, chopped
25g/1oz/2 tbsp unsalted (sweet) butter or
　　non-hydrogenated margarine
45ml/3 tbsp light muscovado (brown) sugar
90g/3½oz/scant 2 cups fresh white or
　　wholemeal (whole-wheat) breadcrumbs
600ml/1 pint/2½ cups double (heavy)
　　cream or soya cream
30ml/2 tbsp unrefined icing
　　(confectioners') sugar
5ml/1 tsp mixed (apple pie) spice
75g/3oz/¾ cup brazil nuts, finely chopped
2–3 bay leaf sprigs, egg white, caster
　　(superfine) sugar or rapadura and
　　fresh cherries, to decorate

1 Put the dried fruit in a food processor and process briefly to chop roughly. Tip the fruit into a bowl and add the port and ginger. Leave to marinate for 2 hours.

2 Melt the butter in a frying pan. Add the muscovado sugar and heat gently until dissolved. Tip in the breadcrumbs and fry gently for 5 minutes. Leave to cool.

3 Tip the breadcrumbs into a food processor and process to finer crumbs. Sprinkle a third into an 18cm/7in loose-based springform tin (pan) and freeze.

4 Whip the cream with the icing sugar and mixed spice to soft peaks. Fold in the nuts and dried fruit mixture.

5 To make sugared bay leaves for decoration, wash and dry the sprigs, then paint both sides with beaten egg white. Dust evenly with sugar. Leave to dry for 2–3 hours.

6 Spread a third of the spiced fruit cream mixture over the frozen breadcrumb base in the tin, taking care not to dislodge any of the crumbs. Sprinkle the cream mixture with another layer of the fine, crispy breadcrumbs. Repeat the layering, finishing with a layer of the spiced fruit cream mixture. Cover the torte with clear film (plastic wrap) and freeze it overnight.

7 Remove the torte from the freezer and place in the refrigerator for about 1 hour before serving, decorated with sugared bay leaves and fresh cherries.

RICOTTA CHEESECAKE

This Sicilian-style cheesecake makes good use of ricotta's firm texture. Here, the cheese is enriched with eggs and cream and enlivened with the unwaxed grated rind of organic orange and lemon producing an irresistible, tangy dessert cheesecake filling.

SERVES EIGHT

450g/1lb/2 cups ricotta cheese
120ml/4fl oz/½ cup double (heavy) cream
  or soya cream
2 eggs
1 egg yolk
75g/3oz/6 tbsp unrefined caster (superfine)
  sugar or rapadura
finely grated rind of 1 orange and 1 lemon,
  plus extra to decorate

For the pastry
175g/6oz/1½ cups plain (all-purpose) flour
45ml/3 tbsp unrefined caster (superfine)
  sugar or rapadura
115g/4oz/½ cup chilled butter, diced
1 egg yolk

1 To make the pastry, sift the flour and sugar on to a cold work surface. Make a well in the centre and add the butter and egg yolk. Work the flour into the butter and egg yolk.

2 Gather the dough together, reserve a quarter of it and press the rest into a 23cm/9in fluted flan tin (quiche pan) with a removable base, and chill.

3 Preheat the oven to 190°C/375°F/ Gas 5. Put the cheese, cream, eggs and egg yolk, sugar and citrus rinds in a large bowl and beat well.

4 Prick the bottom of the pastry case, then line with foil and fill with baking beans. Bake for 15 minutes, transfer to a wire rack, remove the foil and beans and allow the pastry to cool in the tin.

5 Spoon the cheese and cream filling into the pastry case and level the surface. Roll out the reserved dough and cut into long, even strips. Arrange the strips on the top of the filling in a lattice pattern, sticking them in place with water.

6 Bake the cheesecake for 30–35 minutes until golden and set. Transfer to a wire rack and leave to cool, then carefully remove the side of the tin. Use a palette knife (metal spatula) to transfer the tart to a serving plate. Decorate with citrus rind before serving.

VARIATIONS
• Add 50g/2oz/⅓ cup plain chocolate chips to the filling in step 3.
• Scatter 75g/3oz sultanas (golden raisins) into the pastry case before adding the filling.

CAKES AND BAKES

There's something very comforting about cake.

It is universally enjoyed, which is one reason why

the recipes in this section come from all over the globe.

Many of the bakes are traditional, dating back to days when

all food was naturally organic. Russian Poppy Seed Cake,

Greek Fruit and Nut Pastries and Hungarian Fruit Bread

are just some of the delights that are well worth rediscovering.

From Poland comes a Custard Tart topped with juicy plums,

while America is the source of an unusual Butternut Squash

and Maple Pie. Flavoured with fresh organic ginger and

brandy, it is the perfect choice for entertaining.

RUSSIAN POPPY SEED CAKE

This plain and simple cake is based on my mother's recipe. Flavoured with lemon and vanilla, and studded with tiny black organic poppy seeds, it has a nutty, distinctive taste that is utterly delicious.

SERVES ABOUT EIGHT

130g/4½oz/generous 1 cup self-raising (self-rising) flour
5ml/1 tsp baking powder
2 eggs
225g/8oz/generous 1 cup unrefined caster (superfine) sugar or rapadura
5–10ml/1–2 tsp vanilla essence (extract)
200g/7oz/scant 1½ cups poppy seeds, ground
15ml/1 tbsp grated lemon rind
120ml/4fl oz/½ cup milk or soya milk
130g/4½oz/generous ½ cup unsalted (sweet) butter or non-hydrogenated margarine, melted and cooled
30ml/2 tbsp sunflower oil
unrefined icing (confectioners') sugar, sifted, for dusting
whipped cream or soya cream, to serve

1 Preheat the oven to 180°C/350°F/Gas 4. Grease a deep 23cm/9in round springform cake tin (pan). Sift together the flour and baking powder.

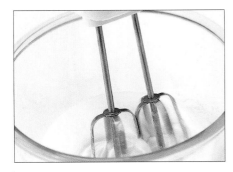

2 Using an electric whisk, beat together the eggs, sugar and vanilla essence for 4–5 minutes until pale and fluffy. Stir in the poppy seeds and the lemon rind.

VARIATION
To make a poppy seed tart, pour the cake mixture into a par-cooked pastry crust, then bake for 30 minutes, or until the filling is firm and risen.

3 Gently fold the sifted ingredients into the egg and poppy seed mixture, in three batches, alternating with the milk, then fold in the melted butter or margarine and sunflower oil.

4 Pour the mixture into the tin and bake for 40 minutes, or until firm. Cool in the tin for 15 minutes, then invert on to a wire rack. Leave until cold, dust with icing sugar and serve with cream.

DOUBLE-GINGER CAKE

Preserved stem ginger and organic root ginger, which is smaller and has a more intense
flavour than the non-organic variety, are used in this tasty tea bread.

SERVES EIGHT TO TEN

3 eggs
225g/8oz/generous I cup unrefined caster
    (superfine) sugar or rapadura
250ml/8fl oz/I cup sunflower oil
5ml/I tsp vanilla essence (extract)
15ml/I tbsp syrup from a jar of preserved
    stem ginger
225g/8oz courgettes (zucchini), grated
2.5cm/1in piece fresh root ginger, peeled
    and finely grated
350g/12oz/3 cups unbleached plain
    (all-purpose) flour
5ml/I tsp baking powder
5ml/I tsp ground cinnamon
2 pieces preserved stem ginger, drained
    and finely chopped
15ml/I tbsp unrefined demerara (raw)
    sugar or rapadura
butter, to serve (optional)

1 Preheat the oven to 190°C/375°F/
Gas 5. Beat together the eggs and sugar
until light and fluffy. Slowly beat in the
oil until the mixture forms a batter.
Mix in the vanilla essence and ginger
syrup, then stir in the grated courgettes
and fresh ginger.

2 Sift together the flour and baking
powder into a large bowl. Add the
cinnamon and mix well, then stir
the dried ingredients into the
courgette mixture.

COOK'S TIP
There is no need to peel fresh organic
root ginger. Special bamboo graters can be
found in many Asian stores, but a simple
box grater will do the job equally well.

3 Lightly grease a 900g/2lb loaf tin (pan)
and pour in the courgette mixture,
making sure it fills the corners. Smooth
and level the top.

4 Mix together the chopped stem ginger
and demerara sugar in a small bowl, then
sprinkle the mixture evenly over the
surface of the courgette mixture.

5 Bake for I hour, or until a skewer
comes out clean when inserted into the
centre. Leave the cake to cool in the
tin (pan) for 20 minutes, then turn out
on to a wire rack and leave to cool
completely. Serve in slices with butter,
if you like.

APRICOT and ALMOND TART

This rich tart relies on a simple but perfect combination of apricots and almond filling.
Fresh apricots are only available during the summer months so make the most of them.

SERVES SIX

115g/4oz/½ cup butter or
    non-hydrogenated margarine
115g/4oz/scant ½ cup unrefined caster
    (superfine) sugar or rapadura
1 egg, beaten
50g/2oz/⅓ cup ground rice
50g/2oz/½ cup ground almonds
few drops of almond essence (extract)
450g/1lb fresh apricots, halved and stoned
sifted unrefined icing (confectioners')
    sugar, for dusting (optional)
apricot slices and fresh mint sprigs,
    to decorate (optional)

For the pastry
115g/4oz/1 cup brown rice flour
115g/4oz/1 cup corn meal
115g/4oz/½ cup butter or
    non-hydrogenated margarine
25g/1oz/2 tbsp unrefined caster (superfine)
    sugar or rapadura
1 egg yolk

1 To make the pastry, place the rice flour and corn meal in a large mixing bowl and stir to mix. Lightly rub in the butter or margarine with your fingertips until the mixture resembles fine breadcrumbs.

VARIATIONS

For a change, use ground hazelnuts and vanilla essence (extract) in place of the ground almonds and almond essence. Pears, peaches or nectarines can be used in this recipe instead of the apricots. Or use a combination of the three fruits to make a mixed fruit tart.

2 Add the sugar, stir in the egg yolk and add enough chilled water to make a smooth, soft but not sticky dough. Wrap the dough in clear film (plastic wrap) and chill for 30 minutes.

3 Preheat the oven to 180°C/350°F/ Gas 4. Line a 24cm/9½in loose-bottomed flan tin (quiche pan) with the pastry by pressing it gently over the base and up the sides of the tin, making sure that there are no holes in the pastry. Trim the edge of the pastry with a sharp knife.

4 To make the almond filling, place the butter or margarine and sugar in a mixing bowl and cream together, using a wooden spoon, until the mixture is light and fluffy.

5 Gradually add the beaten egg to the mixture, beating well after each addition. Fold in the ground rice and almonds and the almond essence and mix well to incorporate them.

6 Spoon the almond mixture into the pastry case, spreading it evenly with the back of a spoon, then arrange the apricot halves cut side down on top.

7 Place the tart on a baking sheet and bake for 40–45 minutes until the filling and pastry are cooked and lightly browned. Serve warm or cold, dusted with icing sugar and decorated with apricots and sprigs of mint, if you like.

COOK'S TIP

Organic apricots are often smaller and are more intensely coloured than non-organic fruit. They have a sweeter, juicier flavour too. Organic apricots, like organic peaches and figs, help regulate the body's digestive system. Try substituting organic peaches and figs in this recipe.

CUSTARD TART with PLUMS

When this tart is made with really ripe, organic sweet plums, it makes a wonderful hot or cold weekend dessert. Serve it with thick cream, ice cream or Greek yogurt.

2 Flour a deep 18cm/7in square or 20cm/8in round loose-bottomed flan tin (tart pan). Roll out the pastry and use to line the tin. This pastry is soft at this stage, so don't worry if you have to push it into shape. Chill for another 10–20 minutes.

3 Preheat the oven to 200°C/400°F/ Gas 6. Line the pastry case with baking parchment and fill with baking beans, then bake for 15 minutes. Remove the paper and baking beans, reduce the oven temperature to 180°C/350°F/Gas 4 and bake for a further 5–10 minutes until the base is dry.

4 Halve and stone the plums, and arrange them neatly in the pastry case. Whisk together the remaining egg and egg yolks with the sugar, the milk and vanilla essence and pour over the fruit.

5 Return the tart to the oven and bake for 25–30 minutes, or until the custard is just firm to the touch. Remove the tart from the oven and allow to cool. Sprinkle with flaked almonds and dredge with icing sugar before serving with cream, ice cream or Greek yogurt.

SERVES FOUR TO SIX

175g/6oz/1½ cups plain (all-purpose) flour, sifted

pinch of salt

45ml/3 tbsp unrefined caster (superfine) sugar or rapadura

115g/4oz/½ cup unsalted (sweet) butter or non-hydrogenated margarine

2 eggs, plus 2 egg yolks

350g/12oz ripe plums

300ml/½ pint/1¼ cups milk or soya milk

few drops of vanilla essence (extract)

toasted flaked (sliced) almonds and sifted unrefined icing (confectioners') sugar, to decorate

1 Place the flour, salt, 15ml/1 tbsp of the sugar, the butter and one of the eggs in a food processor or blender and process until thoroughly combined. Tip out the mixture on to a clean, lightly floured surface and bring it together into a ball. Wrap the pastry in clear film (plastic wrap) and chill for 10 minutes to rest.

VARIATIONS
• This tart is equally delicious made with organic apricots, peaches or nectarines.
• Make a nutty pastry by replacing 15ml/ 1 tbsp of the flour with ground almonds.

BUTTERNUT SQUASH and MAPLE PIE

This American-style pie has a rich shortcrust pastry case and a creamy filling, sweetened
with maple syrup and flavoured with fresh organic ginger and a dash of brandy.

SERVES TEN

1 small butternut squash
60ml/4 tbsp water
2.5cm/1in piece of fresh root ginger,
    peeled and grated
beaten egg, to glaze
120ml/4fl oz/½ cup double (heavy) cream
    or soya cream, plus extra to serve
90ml/6 tbsp maple syrup
45ml/3 tbsp unrefined light muscovado
    (brown) sugar or rapadura
3 eggs, lightly beaten
30ml/2 tbsp brandy
1.5ml/¼ tsp grated nutmeg

For the pastry
175g/6oz/1½ cups plain (all-purpose) flour
115g/4oz/½ cup butter or
    non-hydrogenated margarine, diced
10ml/2 tsp unrefined caster (superfine)
    sugar or rapadura
1 egg, lightly beaten

1 To make the pastry, sift the flour into
a mixing bowl. Rub in the butter or
margarine until the mixture resembles
fine breadcrumbs. Add the sugar and the
egg. Mix to a dough. Wrap in clear film
(plastic wrap). Chill for 30 minutes.

2 Cut the butternut squash in half, then
peel and scoop out the seeds. Cut the
flesh into cubes and put in a pan with
the water. Cover and cook gently for
15 minutes. Remove the lid, stir in the
ginger and cook for a further 5 minutes
until all the liquid has evaporated and
the squash is tender. Cool slightly, then
purée in a food processor until smooth.

3 Roll out the pastry and use to line a
23cm/9in flan tin (tart pan). Gather up
the trimmings, re-roll them thinly, then
cut them into maple-leaf shapes. Brush
the edge of the pastry case with beaten
egg and attach the maple leaf shapes at
regular intervals to make a decorative
rim. Cover with clear film and chill for
30 minutes.

4 Put a heavy baking sheet in the oven
and preheat to 200°C/400°F/Gas 6.
Prick the pastry base with a fork, line
with foil and fill with baking beans. Bake
on the hot baking sheet for 12 minutes.

5 Remove the foil and beans and bake
the pastry case for a further 5 minutes.
Brush the base of the pastry case with
beaten egg and return to the oven for
about 3 minutes. Reduce the oven
temperature to 180°C/350°F/Gas 4.

6 Mix 200g/7oz/scant 1 cup of the
butternut purée with the cream, syrup,
sugar, eggs, brandy and grated nutmeg.
(Discard any remaining purée.) Pour
into the pastry case. Bake for about
30 minutes, or until the filling is lightly
set. Cool slightly, then serve with cream.

FRUIT, NUT AND SEED TEABREAD

Cut into slices and spread with a little butter or non-hydrogenated margarine, jam or honey, this teabread makes an ideal breakfast bread. The dried fruit, nuts and seeds mean it is a fine source of fibre.

MAKES ONE 900G/2LB LOAF

115g/4oz/⅔ cup dried dates, chopped
115g/4oz/½ cup dried apricots, chopped
115g/4oz/1 cup sultanas (golden raisins)
115g/4oz/½ cup unrefined soft light brown
   sugar or rapadura
225g/8oz/2 cups self-raising (self-rising)
   flour
5ml/1 tsp baking powder
10ml/2 tsp mixed (apple pie) spice
75g/3oz/¾ cup chopped mixed nuts
75g/3oz/¾ cup mixed seeds, such as
   linseed, sunflower and sesame seeds
2 eggs, beaten
150ml/¼ pint/⅔ cup semi-skimmed
   (low-fat) milk or soya milk

1 Preheat the oven to 180°C/350°F/ Gas 4. Lightly grease a 900g/2lb loaf tin (pan). Place the chopped dates and apricots and sultanas in a large mixing bowl and stir in the sugar.

COOK'S TIPS
• Use wholemeal (whole-wheat) self-raising (self-rising) flour for an unbeatable nutty flavour.
• Organic dates have an extremely sweet taste, which makes them wonderful to bake with.
• Try adding hemp seeds to the seed mixture for a really nutritious touch.

2 Place the flour, baking powder, mixed spice, mixed nuts and seeds in a separate bowl and mix well.

3 Stir the eggs and milk into the fruit mixture, then add the flour mixture and beat together until well mixed.

4 Spoon the mixture into the prepared tin and level the surface. Bake for about 1 hour until the teabread is firm to the touch and lightly browned.

5 Allow to cool in the tin for a few minutes, then turn out on to a wire rack to cool completely. Serve warm or cold, cut into slices. Wrap the teabread in foil to store.

HUNGARIAN FRUIT BREAD

When dried, many of the nutrients and sugars in fruit are concentrated but so, unfortunately, are any pesticide residues. So, to ensure a clear conscience as you tuck into a slice of this delightful light bread, always use organic dried fruits – a much healthier choice.

SERVES EIGHT TO TEN

sunflower oil, for greasing
7 egg whites
175g/6oz/scant 1 cup unrefined caster
  (superfine) sugar or rapadura
115g/4oz/1 cup flaked (sliced)
  almonds, toasted
115g/4oz/¾ cup sultanas (golden raisins)
grated rind of 1 lemon
165g/5½oz/1⅓ cups plain (all-purpose)
  flour, sifted, plus extra for flouring
75g/3oz/6 tbsp butter or
  non-hydrogenated margarine, melted

1 Preheat the oven to 180°C/350°F/
Gas 4 and grease and flour a 1kg/2¼lb
loaf tin (pan). Whisk the egg whites until
they are very stiff, but not crumbly. Fold
in the sugar gradually, then the flaked,
toasted almonds, sultanas and lemon rind.

2 Fold the flour and butter into the
mixture and tip it into the prepared tin.
Bake for about 45 minutes until well
risen and pale golden brown. Cool for
a few minutes in the tin, then turn out
and serve warm or cold, in slices.

GREEK FRUIT and NUT PASTRIES

These aromatic sweet pastry crescents are packed with walnuts, which are a really rich source of nutrients. Serve with a cup of organic coffee.

3 Meanwhile, to make the filling, mix the honey and coffee. Add the fruit, walnuts and nutmeg. Stir well, cover and leave to soak for at least 20 minutes.

4 Roll out a portion of dough on a lightly floured surface until about 3mm/⅛in thick. Stamp out rounds using a 10cm/4in round cutter.

5 Place a heaped teaspoonful of filling on one side of each round. Brush the edges with a little milk, then fold over and press the edges together to seal. Repeat with the remaining pastry until all the filling is used.

6 Put the pastries on lightly greased baking sheets, brush with milk and sprinkle with caster sugar.

7 Make a steam hole in each with a skewer. Bake for 35 minutes, or until lightly browned. Cool on a wire rack.

MAKES SIXTEEN

60ml/4 tbsp clear honey
60ml/4 tbsp strong brewed coffee
75g/3oz/½ cup mixed dried fruit, chopped
175g/6oz/1 cup walnuts, chopped
1.5ml/¼ tsp freshly grated nutmeg
milk, to glaze
caster (superfine) sugar or rapadura, for sprinkling

For the pastry
450g/1lb/4 cups plain (all-purpose) flour
2.5ml/½ tsp ground cinnamon
2.5ml/½ tsp baking powder
150g/5oz/10 tbsp unsalted (sweet) butter or non-hydrogenated margarine
1 egg
120ml/4fl oz/½ cup chilled milk or soya milk

1 Preheat the oven to 180°C/350°F/Gas 4. To make the pastry, sift the flour, ground cinnamon and baking powder into a bowl. Rub in the butter until the mixture resembles fine breadcrumbs. Make a well in the middle.

2 Beat the egg and chilled milk or soya milk together and add to the well in the dry ingredients. Mix to a soft dough. Divide the dough into two equal pieces and wrap each in clear film (plastic wrap). Chill for 30 minutes.

COOK'S TIP
These traditional Greek pastries are known as *moshopoungia* in Greece. Serve them warm with morning coffee or afternoon tea with a dollop of whipped cream or crème fraîche.

VARIATIONS
Any dried fruit can be used in this recipe – try a combination of the following: sultanas (golden raisins), raisins, currants, apricots, cherries or prunes.

ORANGE and CORIANDER BRIOCHES

The warm spicy flavour of coriander combines particularly well with orange.
Serve these little buns with marmalade for a lazy weekend breakfast.

MAKES TWELVE

225g/8oz/2 cups strong white bread flour
15g/½oz fresh yeast
2.5ml/½ tsp salt
15ml/1 tbsp unrefined caster (superfine)
　　sugar or rapadura
10ml/2 tsp coriander seeds, coarsely ground
grated rind of 1 orange
2 eggs, beaten
50g/2oz/¼ cup unsalted (sweet) butter or
　　non-hydrogenated margarine, melted
1 small egg, beaten, to glaze
shredded orange rind, to decorate (optional)

1 Grease 12 individual brioche tins.
Blend the yeast with 25ml/1½ tbsp tepid
water in a bowl until smooth. Sift the
flour into a mixing bowl and stir in the
yeast, salt, sugar, coriander seeds and
orange rind. Make a well in the centre,
pour in 30ml/2 tbsp hand-hot water, the
eggs and melted butter and beat to
make a soft dough. Turn the dough on
to a lightly floured surface and knead for
5 minutes. Return to the clean, lightly
oiled bowl, cover with clear film (plastic
wrap) and leave in a warm place for
about 1 hour, or until doubled in bulk.

2 Tip the dough out on to a floured
surface, knead briefly and roll into a
sausage shape. Cut into 12 pieces. Break
off a quarter of each piece and set aside.
Shape the larger pieces of dough into
balls and place in the prepared tins.

VARIATION
If you prefer, use 10ml/2 tsp easy-blend
(rapid-rise) dried yeast instead of fresh
yeast, and add to the flour in step 1.

3 With a floured wooden spoon handle,
press a hole in each dough ball. Shape
each small piece of dough into a little
plug and press into the holes.

COOK'S TIP
These little brioches look particularly
attractive if they are made in special
brioche tins. However, they can also be
made in bun or muffin tins.

4 Place the brioche tins on a baking
sheet. Cover with lightly oiled clear film
and leave in a warm place until the
dough rises almost to the top of the tins.
Preheat the oven to 220°C/425°F/Gas 7.
Brush the brioches with beaten egg and
bake for 15 minutes until golden brown.
Scatter over extra shreds of orange rind
to decorate, if you like, and serve the
brioches warm with butter.

GLOSSARY

As in every specialist area, organics has its own language. The following is a guide to some of the specialist terms in common usage.

Agriculture The cultivation of crops and raising of livestock for the production of food and other products.

Agrochemical A chemical or chemical compound used in farming. Also an adjective to describe produce derived from farms that extensively use these chemicals, or the method of agriculture that utilizes agrochemicals.

Aquaculture The farming of fish and other creatures that live in fresh or sea water e.g. salmon and prawns.

Artificial additives Chemicals and chemical compounds added to foods in order to manipulate their taste, colour, texture or shelf life. These include powerful toxins such as tartrazine, a neurotoxin that is used in cordials and soft drinks (sodas) to dye them orange. Only seven of the seven thousand additives used in non-organic food may be used in organic food.

Biodiversity The wide diversity of plants and creatures that occurs in nature.

Also the ideal of organic systems of farming, biodiversity is a term to describe farms rich in different species of plants and animals, whether intentionally cultivated and bred, or those which occur naturally.

Biodynamics Based on the work of the early twentieth century theosophist Rudolph Steiner, biodynamic farming relies on companion planting, homeopathic preparations and a seven-year cycle of crop rotation to remain entirely chemical-free. Biodynamic farms are completely self-contained, integrating different crops and livestock to create a mini-ecosystem. The lunar calendar is used as a guide to planting and harvesting crops, with different star constellations signalling the most fruitful times for these activities. Biodynamics is part of the family of organic farming styles.

Certification Each organic certification board has a different code of standards. However, the basic organic standards are legally defined in international law, so every certification board throughout the world must at least comply with these standards. Check details with each certifier if you want to know if they enforce standard organic standards or stricter ones.

Companion planting A method of growing plants in combinations that optimize their beneficial effects while minimizing their negative effects on each other. For example, growing potatoes near tomatoes weakens their resistance to potato blight, so this should be avoided. Growing chamomile and peppermint in proximity is beneficial, as both plants produce more active essential oils in combination. Companion planting is a practical way of conserving and utilizing biodiversity.

Compost Vegetable and animal matter that has been purposefully decomposed (aerobically fermented) to create a natural source of nutrients for growing crops. Encourages good soil quality and beneficial enzyme production. Organic farmers must follow strict procedures to produce composts and

manures. They compost for lengthy periods to ensure that e-coli and other bugs are killed off. Also extensively manufactured and utilised by organic home gardeners.

Crop rotation A traditional method of effectively managing soil fertility on a farm by systematically rotating crops between different fields. This method often includes leaving fields to lie fallow, meaning that they are rested from production to regain their naturally fertile soil.

Fair trade The concept that a fair price will be paid for goods produced by farmers and workers in the developing world. Many poorer farmers are forced to sell their products for much less than is just if there is no other outlet for them. Fair trade means that a buyer from the developed world will not exploit this opportunity to pay less money than a commodity is worth. Effectively, honourable behaviour rather than exploitation. The official Fairtrade Mark prohibits child and forced labour, and

guarantees that workers receive a decent standard of housing, health and safety protection and employment rights. It also promotes programmes for environmental sustainability.

Fertilizers Generally refers to synthetic chemicals and chemical compounds based on synthetic nitrates used by farmers to give plants extra nutrients for growth. An excess of nitrates is known to cause cancer in humans and animals. Organic farming uses natural fertilizers instead, such as manure, seaweed, clays and rockdust.

Free range A term to describe farm animals and birds that have been able to gain some access to open pastures and skies. When applied to chickens and their eggs, it may simply mean that the chicken house has "popholes" but does not guarantee that the birds will have used these exits, especially if they have been bred in confinement. In the UK the Soil Association has the highest standards for free range poultry and eggs – prohibiting debeaking and overcrowding, and ensuring that all birds range properly in daylight. If in doubt, check with your local certification board for details of their guidelines.

Fungicides Chemicals and chemical compounds used to prevent moulds growing on crops or food products by killing fungal spores. Organic farming prohibits their use. However, where the whole crop might otherwise be lost to something like potato blight or mildew, small amounts of

traditional chemicals, such as copper and sulphur compounds may be used by organic farmers. This practice is restricted to extreme cases, and permission must be granted from an organic certifier.

Gardening The practice of organic gardening is an extremely valuable activity. The United Nations' Food and Agriculture Organisation has calculated that small biodiverse gardens can produce thousands of times more food per acre than large intensive monocultures. Home gardening in Indonesia provides around 40 per cent of all food, and in Eastern Nigeria, the 2 per cent of land cultivated as domestic gardens provides 50 per cent of the food. Gardening provides people in industrialised nations with a connection to the food they eat, whether it is growing herbs in a window box or fruit and vegetables in a garden.

Genetic modification The manipulation of genetic material between different unrelated species of living entities. In agriculture, the creation of crops known as Genetically Modified Organisms (GMOs) or Transgenic Organisms by extracting genes from one species and inserting them in another. GM farming is part of the family of farming styles that makes up agrochemical farming.

GMOs Genetically Modified Organisms (see previous entry).

Herbicides Chemicals and chemical compounds used to kill weeds. Organic farming prohibits their use.

Hydroponics A modern method of agrochemical farming that grows plants in a purely synthetic environment. The plants are suspended in a liquid mixture of nutrient compounds in a medium of sand or gravel. Bright lights are often used to stimulate plant growth. Many non-organic potato and tomato crops are now routinely grown without soil.

Insecticides Chemicals and chemical compounds used to kill insects.

Irradiation The passing of food through a radiation field to preserve it beyond its natural shelf life. The use of ionizing irradiation to preserve food is prohibited under organic standards.

Legumes Crops related to the bean family. Planted extensively in organic agriculture to maintain beneficial levels of nitrogen in the soil. Legumes have the capacity to fix nitrogen from the air into the soil through nodules in their roots. They are often planted as part of the crop rotation system in fallow fields.

Monocultures Agrochemical farms that continually grow only one kind of crop over a vast area. Monocultures are the antithesis of biodiversity, and they are the prevalent form of agriculture in most industrialized nations at the beginning of the 21st century. Four per cent of all farms in the USA produce half of the food grown there on huge swathes of land growing only a single species.

Organic A method of farming based on the cultivation of good soil quality and biodiversity. The use of agrochemicals is strictly regulated and kept to the absolute minimum. It prohibits GMOs (even in animal feed), and is a legally binding term defined in international law. The rearing of organic animals must be according to strict welfare standards, and they may only be treated with chemicals such as antibiotics as a last resort to cure illness. When the term is used to describe a food product or item, at least 95 per cent of its ingredients must be certified organic and it may not be irradiated.

Permaculture This is the design and maintenance of food growing systems which have the diversity, stability, and resilience of natural ecosystems. It is the harmonious integration of the landscape with people, in cities or rural areas. Permaculture can be as small as a city balcony or as large as a forest. It is a way of providing food, energy, shelter and other material and non-material needs in a sustainable way

Pesticides Chemicals and chemical compounds used by farmers and gardeners to kill pests. These products often contain organophosphates, which belong to the same family of chemicals as nerve gases. Synthetic pesticides are applied to crops and livestock as a matter of course in agrochemical agriculture for the prevention and treatment of pests. In organic farming, they may only be applied to crops if all other non-chemical actions to tackle a pest problem have failed, and then only with permission from a certifier. Organic farming relies on biodiversity to provide natural predators to control pests, or uses natural plant-based pesticides. Standards are rigorous and organic farms unfortunate enough to be affected by pesticide drift from neighbouring agrochemical properties have on occasion had their licences revoked.

Prevention The method utilised by organic farmers to minimise the use of agrochemicals, hormones and antibiotics in farming practices. Pesticide use is minimised by careful management, from companion planting to the use of satellite technology to detect potential parasites. Chemical use for livestock is minimised by keeping numbers of animals and fish lower per pen, and encouraging more freedom of movement within the farm or fish tank.

Processed Food Food that has been ready prepared from its raw state for consumption. This can be through a great variety of processes, including boiling, slicing, and baking. Processing food by its very nature removes nutrients and vitality. 70 per cent of all food grown in the USA is processed before it reaches the shops. Only 1 per cent of food grown in India is processed before it is retailed. Indian citizens do not eat their produce raw, but simply process the ingredients themselves at home.

Selective Breeding A traditional genetic technique that produces plants or animals with a particular genetic profile. Reasons may include creating a distinctive taste, unusual colour or hardier variety. It is unrelated to modern genetic modification, as selective breeding takes part between plants of the same species through interbreeding rather than between differing species using DNA displacement technology.

INDEX